FINDING GOD WHEN HE SEEMS TO BE HIDING

INTELLIGENT ANSWERS TO PROFOUND QUESTIONS

KEVIN SIMINGTON

Smart Faith Press

Copyright © 2019 by Kevin Simington

All rights reserved.

No part of this book may be reproduced in any form or by any electronic or mechanical means, including information storage and retrieval systems, without written permission from the author, except for the use of brief quotations in a book review.

Published by SMART FAITH PRESS

SMART FAITH PRESS

ISBN: 978-0-6484945-7-7

❦ Created with Vellum

DEDICATION

To my son, Scott.
May you find the God who made you and loves you.

"You have made us for yourself, O Lord,
and our hearts are restless until they find their rest in You."
Augustine of Hippo, 354 – 430

ACKNOWLEDGMENTS

I would like to thank and honour my wonderful wife, Sandy. She not only stoically endured many long months of being a "book widow", but, once the manuscript was finished, she became my editor. I cannot thank her enough for her meticulous editing, which involved reading through the entire manuscript several times. Her exacting corrections and wise suggestions not only improved the readability of the text, but also transformed the entire direction of the book.

PREFACE

This book arose out of conversations and correspondence with many people over the years who have voiced questions and objections regarding the existence of God. Some were hardened sceptics, while others were earnest seekers. As I have sought to respond to their issues with answers that are Biblically sound and logically reasonable, I have become aware of the lack of any single published work that deals comprehensively and adequately with the most commonly raised objections:

- *There is no clear evidence for God's existence.*
- *If God exists, why isn't He more obvious?*
- *How can an all-powerful, loving God exist when there is so much suffering and evil in the world?*
- *Jesus is a myth and His resurrection is a complete fabrication.*
- *The Bible is historically unreliable, and full of embellishments and fabrications.*

- *Hypocrisy and sexual abuse has turned me off Christianity for good!*
- *Religion promotes hatred, bigotry and violence.*
- *Hasn't evolution disproved the existence of God?*
- *How can a loving God torture people for eternity in Hell?*
- *If we are incapable of not sinning (as the Bible says) why does God still punish us for something we can't help?*
- *If sin will no longer be possible in Heaven, yet people will still have free wills, why didn't God create a world like this in the first place?*
- *What kind of narcissistic God creates us and demands that we love Him, then tortures those who refuse? What sort of insecurity must God have, that He cannot tolerate people not loving Him?*

While there are reams of verbiage in existence on some of these topics, an alarmingly large proportion of it does not address the issues at a depth that would satisfy an intelligent enquirer. There is certainly no single source where these issues are addressed with the academic rigour, Biblical integrity and philosophical depth that they demand. For these issues are, indeed, profound and cannot be dismissed with a light sprinkling of glib answers. This book, therefore, was born out of necessity; the need to provide substantial answers to each of these questions in a single, cohesive volume.

In the course of writing this book, some of my own beliefs, particularly regarding the concept of an eternal Hell, have undergone a transformation. The serious objections raised by seekers and sceptics have forced me to go back to the Scriptures and examine the issues with a hermeneutical diligence that I had not previously employed on some of these topics. Despite 4 years of theological training and 35 years of full-time Christian ministry, I have reached the surprising conclusion that some of my long-held beliefs were founded upon hermeneutically flawed exegesis. My findings were surprising and liberating, and have led me to a deeper appreciation of the character of God. I will not pre-empt those findings here, for it is a journey that must be undertaken carefully and incrementally.

This book is intensely pastoral in nature. It seeks to provide clear answers for earnest seekers and puzzled Christians. Of course, any discussion of issues such as the origin of evil, the problem of suffering, the nature of free will, the nature of God and the fairness of His actions cannot avoid dipping into theological and philosophical profundity, for these are complex issues. Yet I have attempted to so "dip" while retaining a resolute focus on making these issues understandable for the ordinary reader.

It is my prayer and heart's desire that, through reading this book, your mind will be enlightened, your faith will be strengthened, and you will develop an unshakeable confidence in the unimpeachable character of a just and loving God.

ONE

SEEKING ANSWERS

There is an ancient fable of a young man who set out to find God. He read all the philosophical works that he could find. He travelled the world, interviewing religious leaders and sages. Finally, after years of fruitless searching, he heard of a wise old monk who lived alone on top of an isolated mountain and decided to visit him. The young man climbed the mountain and found the elderly monk sitting quietly on the front porch of his simple log cabin. The young man stood before the monk and said, *"Old man, I have a problem, and I have been told that you may be able to help me."* The elderly monk replied, *"What is your problem?"* The young man responded, *"I am searching for God. I have spent the last few years travelling the world and I cannot find Him anywhere."* The wise old monk remained silent for some time, gazing out at the magnificent vista of mist-filled valleys and mountain tops painted gold by the setting sun. Eventually, he turned to the young man and said, *"Young man, I have the opposite problem."* The puzzled young man asked, *"What is it?"* The monk replied, *"I can't **not** see God."*

I have that old monk's problem. I can't **not** see God. I see evidence of His creative hand everywhere. I sense His presence in everything; from the mundane to the majestic, from the simple to the sublime. The miracle of birth, the infinite splendour of the stars, the beauty of a sunset, the colour of a flower, the smell of the ocean and the simple joy of holding the hand of someone I love. These, and a million other things, constantly affirm to me the existence of an infinitely powerful Creator God. I have never had a problem believing in God; I don't think I have ever seriously doubted His existence.

But I have had many questions. There is a difference between questions and doubt. Questions reveal a lack of understanding; doubt reveals a lack of belief. Most Christians have belief tempered with questions. This is normal and, in some ways, unavoidable, because we are finite beings attempting to understand an infinite God. There will inevitably be questions that will puzzle and even perplex us; questions concerning the nature of God and His dealings with mankind. Some of these questions will remain unanswered for our entire lives, only finding resolution when we are finally ushered into God's eternal Kingdom. Other questions will gradually resolve themselves as we grow closer to God and as we delve deeper into His Word. This book provides helpful answers to many of the questions that perplex and confuse Christians.

This book also seeks to help those who do not yet believe in God; those who have doubts about the very existence of God.

Over the years I have had many conversations with people who are earnestly seeking to believe in God, but who are plagued by doubts; doubts fuelled by serious questions that form seemingly insurmountable obstacles to faith. In my encounters with both earnest seekers and hardened sceptics alike, I have realised that there are only a small number of questions and objections that are commonly articulated. Here is a brief summary of the most common questions and objections posed by seekers and sceptics:

COMMON QUESTIONS AND OBJECTIONS

- *There is no clear evidence for God's existence.*
- *If God exists, why isn't He more obvious?*
- *How can an all-powerful, loving God exist when there is so much suffering and evil in the world?*
- *Jesus is a myth and His resurrection is a complete fabrication.*
- *The Bible is historically unreliable, and full of embellishments and fabrications.*
- *Hypocrisy and sexual abuse has turned me off Christianity for good!*
- *Religion promotes hatred, bigotry and violence.*
- *Hasn't evolution disproved the existence of God?*
- *How can a loving God torture people for eternity in Hell?*
- *If we are incapable of not sinning (as the Bible says) why does God still punish us for something we can't help?*
- *If sin will no longer be possible in Heaven, yet*

people will still have free wills, why didn't God create a world like this in the first place?
- *What kind of narcissistic God creates us and demands that we love Him, then tortures those who refuse? What sort of insecurity must God have, that He cannot tolerate people not loving Him?*

These are not easy questions to answer, and I suspect that most of us have, at least occasionally, entertained similar questions and doubts.

DIFFERENTIATING BETWEEN CONTRADICTION AND PARADOX

The first step in trying to resolve some of these questions and objections is to understand the difference between a contradiction and a paradox. For example, the claim that a loving God and the existence of suffering in our world are mutually incompatible, assumes an inherent logical contradiction between the two. But this assumption fails to distinguish the difference between a contradiction and a paradox. Contradiction refers to the logical impossibility of two opposing precepts being true at the same time. For example, I cannot be a genius imbecile. I may be a genius (IQ of 140+) or I may be an imbecile (IQ of between 20-49), or I may be neither, but I cannot be both at the same time. A contradiction infers that at least one of the precepts is fallacious, because it is a logical impossibility for them both to be true simultaneously.

A paradox, on the other hand, is when two things have the appearance of incompatibility, but their reconciliation is not logically impossible in an absolute sense. Often a paradox is the result of insufficient contextual information which, if provided, could resolve the paradox. There are many types of paradox (self-referencing, vicious circularity, infinite regress, etc), but the one we are concerned with here is the contextual paradox. An example of this would be the statement: *"I love my dog, so I cut off his back leg."* Superficially, this statement seems internally contradictory. The cruelty of removing a limb seems incongruent with the owner's professed love. But if additional contextual information is provided, (that the leg was cancerous and would have led to the eventual demise of the dog), the paradox is resolved. Of course, not all paradoxes are so easily resolved. Some paradoxes may not be resolved in one lifetime, or even in many, but one has the sense that they are not beyond the realm of solvability. In the case of the apparent incompatibility between the existence of a loving, all-powerful God and the presence of suffering in our world, or between a loving God and the existence of Hell, could there be additional information, of which we are currently unaware, or only dimly aware, which could resolve the paradox?

The claim that a just and loving God could not possibly have a morally defensible reason for allowing suffering in our world or for sending people to a torturous Hell – that a loving God and these realities are absolutely contradictory - assumes that there are no possible contextualising factors that could reconcile the two. Additionally, the claim of irreconcilable contradiction assumes that the one claiming the contradiction has had access to all possible knowledge in the universe that could pertain to the issue. It assumes that the questioner has assessed all possible scenarios and permutations, thereby reaching the absolute conclusion that a loving God and suffering, for example, cannot possibly co-exist. Surely this is hubris in the extreme; arrogance of the highest order! Given the fact that none of us are omniscient (all-knowing), the claim of absolute, irreconcilable incompatibility in this issue simply cannot be made.

THE POSSIBILITY OF INSCRUTABLE HIGHER PURPOSES

If we assume that the God who created the universe is a transcendent being whose wisdom and power are infinitely greater than ours, (which is a reasonable assumption, given the mind-boggling scale and grandeur of the universe), then it would be naive in the extreme to presume that His purposes and thought processes would be completely discernible and understandable to limited creatures such as ourselves. In fact, the scenario with the highest probability is that any God who is capable of creating all the matter in the universe from nothing - who is able to design billions of galaxies with quadrillions of stars across an expanse of untold billions of lightyears - will be so incomprehensively superior to us, that our feeble brains will be incapable of apprehending all but the vaguest notions of His nature and His purposes.

This is precisely the point that God made to the Israelites through the prophet Isaiah;

"For my thoughts are not your thoughts, neither are your ways my ways," declares the Lord. "As the heavens are higher than the earth, so are my ways higher than your ways and my thoughts than your thoughts" (Isa 55:8-9).

In other words, if this transcendent God is infinitely powerful and infinitely wise, it follows that many of His purposes and actions will be infinitely beyond our ability to comprehend. We have less chance of completely understanding God than an ant has of understanding astrophysics! The possibility of inscrutable higher purposes undergirding the existence of suffering or the existence of Hell are, therefore, deducibly certain.

THE LIMITS OF SPECULATION

Mankind's ignorance of God's infinitely higher purposes not only renders the arguments of His accusers insubstantial, but also places severe limits on any proposed explanations by His defenders. While the Bible does provide a significant amount of contextual doctrine that can bring us to a fundamental grasp of the key concept of salvation and of God's dealings with mankind, we are effectively only paddling in the shallows of these issues. The infinite God has revealed to us those things that we need to know in order to be saved, but there is much that we have not been told, either because such knowledge would be unhelpful or because we are incapable of understanding it. This means that any discussion which attempts to move beyond the basic descriptions of the Bible will necessarily remain speculative.

THE TEMPORARY NATURE OF HUMAN IGNORANCE

The Bible promises that our current state of ignorance, however, is a temporary one. When we leave this life and enter the eternal dimension that awaits the children of God, our current cognitive limitations will dissipate. In 1 Corinthians 13:12, we read, *"For now we see only a reflection as in a mirror;*

then we shall see face to face. Now I know in part; then I shall know fully, even as I am fully known." While there are some who interpret this verse to be anticipatory of the enhanced understanding that would follow from the completion of the New Testament Scriptures, the overwhelming majority of Biblical scholars interpret this to be the promise of complete enlightenment in God's eternal Kingdom. This eschatological (future) interpretation is the most internally consistent, particularly in the light of verse 10, which looks ahead to *"when the fulfilment of all things comes"*. In other words, the things that are unclear now will one day be crystal clear. The things that we currently perceive dimly and in part, we will eventually understand with acuity and in full. This does not infer that we will be granted omniscience, the perfect knowledge of all things everywhere, but simply that all our questions and possible lines of enquiry will be fully answered. Everything will finally make perfect sense.

Although the sceptic who believes in neither God nor life after death will derive no comfort from this line of reasoning, it still carries relevance for our discussion of many of the questions and objections dealt with in this book. This promise of eventual enlightenment indicates that God wants us to eventually reach complete understanding on these issues. He wants to answer our questions. The fact that He presently withholds those answers may be for a variety of reasons. In some cases, it may be that certain information would be currently unhelpful for us. In other cases, it may be that we are currently incapable of understanding some concepts. Alternatively, it may simply be that answering every question we have about every aspect of the spiritual realm is not particularly high on God's current to-do list. He is happy to leave certain things in abeyance for the present, so that we may focus on the essential elements of the Gospel and not be overloaded with information. Whatever the reasons, the result is that there are certain things that are only vaguely revealed in Scripture at the present time, and these remain mysterious to us. We are three-dimensional beings trying to envisage a trans-dimensional reality, and until we enter that reality ourselves, it will remain shrouded in mystery.

THE VALIDITY OF SPECULATION

This does not mean that it is inappropriate to speculate. While only limited information is available to us via general revelation in Scripture, God has also equipped us with intellects. The varying levels of mental acuity within humanity, mean that some people are able to probe the mists of uncertainty and make connections where others only perceive darkness. That God enables some among us to reach profound conclusions is, in my opinion, beyond question. The gifts of wisdom and knowledge, listed among the other gifts in 1 Corinthians 12:8, point us in this direction. Some Christians view those particular gifts as operating in a passive, mechanical fashion, whereby God "downloads" specific wisdom and knowledge into the quiescent minds of the recipients. While God may choose to do this on occasions, these gifts normally operate more organically, involving the coalescence of human reasoning with the wisdom of God's Spirit. The ability to ponder profound philosophical and theological truths - to think abstractly about such things as meaning and purpose and justice and love and truth - is a gift from God. And some people are particularly gifted in doing so. This is what sets us apart from the animals; it is part of what it means to be created in God's image.

Our God-given ability to discover truth through abstract thought is evident in many areas of life. We see this, for example, in the sciences. Dr. Paul Davies, in his book, *"Are We Alone?"*, comments:

"The most striking product of the human mind is mathematics. This is a baffling thing. Mathematics is not something that you find lying around in your backyard! It's a product of the human mind. Yet if we ask where mathematics works best, it is in areas like particle physics and astrophysics, areas of fundamental science that are very, very far removed from everyday affairs."[1]

Davies' point is that God has created within us an innate ability to discover truth through abstract thought – truth that allows us to decode the physical universe and reach a profound understanding of its nature and function. The laws and constants of science - the gravitational constant, the speed of light, the cosmological constant, the weak and strong nucleic coupling constants, the Planck constants, and many more – were not given to us in a chapter of the Bible entitled *"Stuff You Need To Know About How The Universe Works"*. God created us with incredible minds, and then effectively said, *"Now go and discover the truth about the amazing universe that I have created!"*. Speaking of mankind's ability to discover and comprehend the universe, Davies concludes;

"I think it is an astonishing and unexpected thing, and it suggests to me that consciousness and our ability to do mathematics is no mere accident, no trivial detail, no insignificant by-product of evolution ... It points to what I like to call the cosmic

connection, the existence of a really deep relationship between minds that can think abstractly and the natural world."[2]

The point I am making here is that God invites us to use our minds to search for truth, and we should not think that this is limited to the physical realm. He does not say to us, *"Use your minds to discover truth in the physical world, but please switch them off in regard to the spiritual realm."* While it is true that the Bible is God's final revelation to mankind, it is by no means an exhaustive one. It is full of clues, hints and obscure passing references to tantalising truths and puzzling concepts. The God who invites us to discover and understand the physical universe, invites us to embark on the same journey in regard to the spiritual realm. He urges us to *"seek"* and *"search"* (Matt 7:7; Jer 29:13). He invites us to use our minds, the minds He has gifted us with, to search for spiritual truth and to seek a deeper understanding of His character and of the spiritual realm that surrounds us.

And so, we begin.

As we continue, we will sometimes ponder eternal issues that are only briefly described in Scripture. We will attempt to join the dots and construct a picture that makes sense. We will seek to understand the nature and purposes of God and His dealings with humanity. And we will do so humbly acknowledging our limitations and, ultimately, trusting in the goodness of God that has been unequivocally revealed to us through the sacrificial death and resurrection of His Son.

Reflection Questions

1. What new insight have you gained from this chapter?

2. What questions or challenges has this chapter raised for you?

3. What is your current view regarding the problem of suffering? How do you reconcile this with the existence of an all-powerful, loving God?

4. Read Isaiah 55:8-11. What is this passage effectively saying? What relevance does it have for our consideration of the nature and purpose of Hell?

5. Read 1 Corinthians 13:9-12. What do you think it means that we will "know fully" and "see face to face"? Does this mean that we will know everything? When will this take place?

6. Read Matthew 13:10-15. Why doesn't God explain everything to us in detail? What is this passage saying about the way God reveals truth to mankind?

TWO

EVIDENCE FOR BELIEF

Over the years I have encountered many earnest seekers and sceptics who claim that there is insufficient evidence to prove the existence of God – and I completely agree with them! You cannot indisputably prove the existence of God. In fact, final and irrevocable proof of anything is impossible. Philosophically speaking, I cannot prove that I exist. I cannot even prove that the physical universe exists; that it is not some giant simulation into which I am plugged. For the most part, we must satisfy ourselves, not with indisputable proof, but with the weight of reasonable evidence which leads us to conclude that something is probably true. The same is true in regard to God. While I cannot indisputably prove His existence, the weight of observable evidence leads me to conclude that the most likely explanation of that evidence is the existence of an all-powerful Creator God.

Of course, sceptics dispute either the fact of this evidence or its significance. They argue that much of the evidence commonly proposed by God's defenders is either weak or has convincing alternate explanations. Consequently, many sceptics claim that if God does exist, and their unbelief ultimately turns out to be wrong, they cannot be blamed for their unbelief – the fault lies with God for not making the evidence for His existence more convincing! In other words, many sceptics claim that they cannot be held culpable (to blame) for their unbelief if it turns out that they are wrong, and God would be unjust for punishing them for their honest mistaken unbelief.

Acclaimed theologian and philosopher, William Lane Craig, answers this objection by proposing that *"there is no such thing as non-culpable, reasonable unbelief."*[1] He contends that there is sufficient evidence for God's existence if one searches with an open heart and mind. According to this view, those who reject that evidence are entirely culpable due to their hard hearts, and God is justified in condemning them. Sceptics, however, argue that reasonable non-belief does exist. They claim that there are many sincere people who have searched for God and failed to find Him. So, the crucial question appears to be, *"Is there such a thing as reasonable, non-culpable unbelief?"*

For the purposes of this discussion, I shall include those who have never heard of God and the Christian message. Whether people have heard of God and of Jesus Christ, and have failed to find any convincing supporting evidence, or whether they have not heard the Christian message at all, the result is the same; they do not believe in God and therefore cannot be said to be wilfully rebelling against Him. This is the argument proposed by sceptics.

THE RARITY OF TRUE ATHEISM

On June 24th, 1982, a British Airways Boeing 747 bound for Australia out of Jakarta was cruising at 12,000 metres over the Indian Ocean, when suddenly, without any warning, all four of its engines failed. For the next 12 minutes the pilots fought desperately to restart them, and the plane plummeted 8,000 meters. For the 263 passengers and crew, it was the longest 12 minutes of their lives, and they were convinced they were about to die. But finally, the Boeing Rolls Royce Engines refired, the pilots managed to pull the plane up out of its dive, and about half an hour later the plane landed back at Jakarta airport. An enquiry found that the engines had stopped because the plane had flown into an invisible cloud of volcanic gas from Mt Galunggung, which was erupting 170 kms away, in West Java. With the gas in the air there was insufficient oxygen to support engine combustion, and so the engines simply stopped! Only after the plane emerged from the gas cloud at 4,000 metres, were the engines finally able to be restarted.

This terrifying event became known as the *"Jakarta Incident"*, and it made world headlines. One of the passengers later published a book on the incident, entitled *"All Four Engines Have Failed"*, and, in 2007, the Discovery Channel Canada and National Geographic produced a TV documentary about it, called *"Falling From The Sky"*[2].

There are two really interesting aspects to the incident. The first is what was happening in the cockpit during those 12 minutes. The crew went through the start-up procedure 67 times before the engines finally restarted. Their remarkable calmness and diligence in following the set procedures has become the classic case study in how to persistently follow procedures during an emergency, and this incident is now quoted and studied in just about every pilot training program around the world.

But what fascinates me most about this story, is what took place in the passenger compartment during those 12 long minutes. It all began with an announcement over the cabin speakers: *"Ladies and gentlemen, this is your captain speaking. We have a small problem. All four engines have stopped. We are doing our damnedest to get them going again. I trust you are not in too much distress."* Many of the passengers later acknowledged that they were convinced they were about to die. Some of them got their passports out of their overhead luggage and placed them in their coat pockets so that their bodies could be properly identified. Several women confessed to putting on stilettoes, just in case they survived, so they could kick the sharks with their heels! The most common response, however, was prayer; desperate, pleading prayer as people cried out to God to save them.

When these praying passengers were later interviewed, they were asked, *"Do you believe in God?"*, and many of them replied that they didn't really have a faith in God.[3] When asked about this inconsistency, some of them explained that it was a natural response arising from their sheer terror. This is certainly not unique. It is not uncommon for people who are professed atheists or agnostics to cry out to God in desperation when they find themselves in terrifying or traumatic circumstances. Atheist, J.D. Moyer, in his article, *"Why, As An Athe-*

ist, I Pray",⁴ speaks of enjoying the experience of feeling as though he is *"talking to someone more powerful than us, who loves us"*. He says that *"prayer can satisfy a sort of psychological craving ... an inner void"*. Furthermore, he states that he does not believe in God, and he acknowledges that *"the entity I'm addressing exists only in my mind — a construct, yet it feels like I'm addressing someone outside of myself — an externality"*.

Both the British Airways incident and J.D. Moyer's admission about his prayer life, illustrate a central truth of Romans 1; that humanity has an innate sense of God's existence, which many people choose to supress:

"... people, who suppress the truth by their wickedness, since what may be known about God is plain to them, because God has made it plain to them." (Rom 1:18-19).

According to the Bible, those who profess to be atheists - either soft atheists (*"I don't believe in God"*) or hard atheists (*"there is no God"*) - are supressing an instinctive awareness of God's existence that He has placed within each of us. Of course, as this innate awareness is supressed over a long period of time by increasing layers of rationalisation, it grows increasingly dimmer. The determined atheist, through the persistent iteration of a dissenting viewpoint and the accumulation of layers of rational counter-argument, can all but extinguish this spark of spiritual awareness. Romans 1 refers to this process as the darkening of the heart:

"For although they knew God, they neither glorified him as God nor gave thanks to him, but their thinking became futile and their foolish hearts were darkened. Although they claimed to be wise, they became fools" (Rom 1:21-22).

The fact that atheists sometimes cry out to God in moments of extreme danger, however, indicates that the spark of spiritual awareness is never completely extinguished. In moments of mortal terror, the carefully constructed layers of disbelief can be stripped away in an instant, revealing the primal, instinctive awareness of God that has never completely deserted them.

Many atheists, if they read this, would, no doubt, strongly disagree with this concept of an intrinsic, universal concept of God within humanity. They would argue that they have no such inner sense of God's presence and that their atheism is untainted by even the slightest equivocation. Yet, history is replete with ardent atheists who, when placed in extreme mortal danger, execute spiritual backflips that would make any gymnast proud.

- **Thomas Paine** (1737-1809) was an English–American political activist, one of the founding fathers of America, and a very outspoken and influential atheist. He published the book, *"The Age Of Reason"*, which was an atheist manifesto that influenced thousands of people to question God's existence. As he lay dying, however, he uttered these famous words, *"I would give worlds if I had them, that The Age of Reason had never been published. O Lord, help me! Christ, help me! No, don't leave; stay with me! For I am on the edge of Hell here! If ever the Devil had an agent, I have been that one."*[5]
- **Sir Frances Newport** (1555 – 1623) was the founding president of the British Infidel Association. As he lay dying, several members of the Association had gathered around his bed, to

encourage and support him. Suddenly, Newport called out, with a look of terror in his eyes, *"You need not tell me there is no God for now I know there is one, and that I am in His presence! You need not tell me there is no Hell. I feel myself already slipping. Wretches, cease your idle talk! I know I am lost forever! Oh, that fire! Oh, the insufferable pangs of Hell!"*[6] He then slumped into unconsciousness and died.

- **Sir Thomas Scott** (1535 – 1594) was an outspoken atheist and member of the British Parliament who was instrumental in passing several laws that were detrimental to the Church in Great Britain at that time. As he lay dying, he cried out, *"Until this moment, I thought there was neither God nor Hell; now I know and feel that there are both, and I am doomed to perdition by the just judgment of the Almighty!"*[7]

- **Voltaire** (1694 – 1778) was a famous French philosopher and an outspoken atheist. His real name was Francois Arouet, but was he better known by his non-deplume, Voltaire. His atheistic writings influenced thousands of people to abandon religious faith. On his death bed, he cried out these final words to his attending physician, "I am abandoned by God and man! I would give you half of what I am worth if you would give me six months life. But I am going to Hell! Oh Christ! Oh Jesus Christ!"[8]

These are some of the more extreme examples of how

mortal terror and the imminence of death can bring a long-buried awareness of God to the surface, one that has been denied and supressed by years of rationalisation, but which is still innately present in the subconscious. I also suspect that as these men lay dying, poised between this realm and the next, they began to glimpse their fate, as if a door to the afterlife began to open as the door to this life closed.

Is there such a thing as indubitable, unequivocal atheism? Many atheists would vehemently declare so. Yet it is the Bible's proposition that even the most emphatic declarations of unbelief, sincerely held by many atheists, represent an unwillingness to attend to the innate sense of God that He has placed within us all. Such people *"suppress the truth ... since what may be known about God is plain to them, because God has made it plain to them"* (Rom 1:19). While atheists may convince themselves of their absolute unbelief, they do not convince God, who declares that, *"people are without excuse"* (Rom 1:20). According to God, there is no such thing as non-culpable unbelief.

So that we are in no doubt as to the culpability of all who disbelieve in God, the first three chapters of the book of Romans explain the precise means by which *"God has made it plain to them"* (Rom 1:19). These early chapters speak of two *"voices"* by which God speaks to the human soul, indicating clearly to us His existence and our need to worship and obey Him.

THE VOICE OF CREATION

"For since the creation of the world God's invisible qualities—His eternal power and divine nature—have been clearly seen,

being understood from what has been made, so that people are without excuse." (Romans 1:20).

The beauty and complexity of creation testifies to the existence of God. Through the wonder of the physical universe, *"His eternal power and divine nature have been clearly seen."* The voice of creation is not a subtle whisper; it cries out in vociferous exclamation! Thousands of years ago, King David wrote, *"The heavens declare the glory of God; the skies proclaim the work of his hands. Day after day they pour forth speech; night after night they reveal knowledge. They have no speech, they use no words; no sound is heard from them. Yet their voice goes out into all the earth, their words to the ends of the world."* (Psalm 19:1-4). The grandeur of the physical universe, with its billions of galaxies and its unspeakable beauty, cries out to humanity in a language that bypasses mere vocabulary and interacts directly with our hearts and souls. It declares to us, day by day, moment by moment, that there is a Creator. The heavens truly do *"declare the glory of God"*.

Of course, atheists disagree with this conclusion. Sam Harris, in his *"Letter To A Christian Nation"*, declares that *"nature offers no compelling evidence for an intelligent designer."* [9] He echoes the opinion of many atheists who fail to be convinced by the evidence of apparent design in nature. This is hardly surprising, as we have already examined the testimony of Scripture regarding mankind's remarkable ability to supress the truth and drown out the voice of God. The Bible, however, is adamant that the evidence for God's existence is overwhelming for those who dare to examine it with open hearts and minds.

The debate concerning the evidence for God's existence, or lack of it, within the natural realm, is an ancient one. Volumes have been written on the topic at the most profound scientific levels. As an interested spectator in the debate myself, regularly reading physics, cosmology, chemistry and genetics, I have noted a dramatic shift in the balance of the debate in recent decades. Recent scientific discoveries and developments have tended to undermine the atheist cause and bolster the evidential case for intelligent design. These developments include:

- Cosmological evidence that the universe had a beginning; that matter came into existence by an unknown means at some point in the distant past.
- Teleological evidence of intelligent design in the natural world, including the statistically impossible fine tuning of the cosmic constants, without which all life, including matter itself, could not exist.
- The impossibility of genetic replication creating new genetic information necessary for the creation of new, modified species, and the equal impossibility of genetic replication errors producing positive mutations; both of which are essential to the theory of evolution.
- The now widely acknowledged complete failure of the fossil record to provide paleontological evidence for macro evolution (major changes from one species to another).

In the area of Cosmology, for example, recent discoveries have had a profound impact on the creation / evolution debate. Until mid-way through last century, atheists have posited that the universe has always existed. Bertrand Russell, the notable atheist (1872 – 1970), stated, *"The universe is just there, and that's all!"*[10] Some remarkable developments over the last century, however, have led the way in overturning this once strongly held presupposition. These developments include extrapolations from Einstein's Theory of Relativity (by Georges Lemaitre and Alexander Friedmann)[11], Edwin Hubble's doppler red shift discoveries (1929)[12], the discovery of cosmic microwave background radiation (CMBR) by Arno Penzias and Robert Wilson in 1964[13], and the more recent measurements of unexpected ambient temperatures of inter-quasar space[14].

These and other discoveries have led the vast majority of the world's leading scientists to conclude that our universe had a beginning, and that matter itself came into existence from nothing! As Stephen Hawking stated, *"All the evidence seems to indicate that the universe has not existed forever, but that it had a beginning. This is probably the most remarkable discovery of modern cosmology."*[15]

The consequence of this is that there are a growing number of the world's most respected scientists who, when faced with the impossibility of the universe popping into existence from nothing of its own accord, are reluctantly conceding that a *"supernatural"* (beyond nature) first cause is the most tenable explanation for the origin of the universe.

Dr Robert Jastrow, astronomer, physicist and founder of NASA's Goddard Institute of Space Studies, states,

"Astronomers now find that they have painted themselves into a corner because they have proven, by their own methods, that the world began abruptly in an act of creation to which you can trace the seeds of every star, every planet, every living thing in this cosmos and on the earth. And they have found that all this happened as a product of forces they cannot hope to discover....

That there are what I or anyone would call supernatural forces at work is now, I think, a scientifically proven fact."[16]

Although this paradigm shift is not yet reflected in popular media, the concept of a "supernatural" (beyond nature) first cause is gaining significant momentum within scientific circles.

In the area of teleology (the study of the purposeful characteristics of the natural world), the apparent fine tuning of the universe provides significant evidence for intelligent design. The fundamental forces or constants of the universe are so extraordinarily fine-tuned for life, that scientists are beginning to concede that they could not have occurred by chance. The 34 recognised universal constants are so finely tuned that altering one by even one thousandth of one percent would render life and, in the case of some of the constants, the existence of matter itself, impossible. Dr. Robin Collins, Professor of Theoretical Physics, North Western University, states, *"The chance of just two of these cosmological constants developing by sheer chance, is one in 100 million trillion trillion trillion trillion trillion trillion. That's more than the number of atoms in the universe! And that's just TWO of the constants!"*.[17] Dr Paul Davies, Professor of Theoretical Physics, Adelaide University, states, *"The physical universe is put together with an ingenuity that is so astonishing, with physical constants that are so impossibly perfect, that I can no longer accept it as the product of brute chance"*.[18]

Table of Universal Constants:[19]

Quantity	Symbol	Numerical value	Unit
Acceleration of free fall (standard)	g_n	9.8066	m s^{-2}
Atmospheric pressure (standard)	p_0	1.0132×10^5	Pa
Atomic mass unit	u	1.6606×10^{-27}	kg
Avogadro constant	N_A	6.0220×10^{23}	mol^{-1}
Bohr magneton	μ_B	9.2741×10^{-24}	J T^{-1}, A m^2
Boltzmann constant	k	1.3807×10^{-23}	J K^{-1}
Electron			
charge	$-e$	1.6022×10^{-19}	C
mass	m_e	9.1095×10^{-31}	kg
charge/mass ratio	e/m_e	1.7588×10^{11}	C/kg
Faraday constant	F	9.6485×10^4	C/mol
Free space			
electric constant	ε_0	8.8542×10^{-12}	F m^{-1}
intrinsic impedance	Z_0	376.7	Ω
magnetic constant	μ_0	$4\pi \times 10^{-7}$	H m^{-1}
speed of electromagnetic waves	c	2.9979×10^8	m/s
Gravitational constant	G	6.6732×10^{-11}	N m^2 kg^{-2}
Ideal molar gas constant	R	8.3144	J/(mol K)
Molar volume at s.t.p.	V_m	2.2414×10^{-2}	m^3/mol
Neutron rest mass	m_n	1.6748×10^{-27}	kg
Planck constant	h	6.6262×10^{-34}	J s
normalised	$h/2\pi$	1.0546×10^{-34}	J s
Proton			
charge	$+e$	1.6022×10^{-19}	C
rest mass	m_p	1.6726×10^{-27}	kg
charge/mass ratio	e/m_p	0.9579×10^{8}	C/kg
Radiation constants	c_1	3.7418×10^{-16}	W m^2
	c_2	1.4388×10^{-2}	m K
Rydberg constant	R_H	1.0968×10^7	m^{-1}
Stefan-Boltzmann constant	σ	5.6703×10^{-8}	J (m^2 K^4)
Wien constant	k_w	2.8978×10^{-3}	m K

The teleological argument for the existence of God is extremely convincing. Dr. Fred Hoyle, astrophysicist and mathematician, Cambridge University, states,

"*A common sense interpretation of the facts suggests that a super-intellect has monkeyed with physics, as well as with chemistry and biology, and that there are no blind forces worth speaking about in nature. The numbers one calculates from the facts seem to me so overwhelming as to put this conclusion almost beyond question.*"[20]

Even Charles Darwin, long before many of these modern discoveries had been made, conceded the strong evidence for intelligent design in the natural world when he spoke of "*the impossibility of conceiving this immense and wonderful universe as the result of blind chance or necessity. I feel compelled to look to a First Cause having an intelligent mind, and I deserve to be called a Theist.*"[21] (Darwin's theism, however, fell short of belief in a personal God. In regard to that aspect, he identified himself as an agnostic).

Of course, determined atheism will never be defeated by rational argument or evidence, no matter how convincing it is, because atheism, at its heart, is spiritual blindness. It is a resolute unwillingness to believe in God; an unwillingness that refuses to see the imprint of the Creator in creation; an unwillingness that grasps desperately at any conceivable alternate explanation for life that enables the unbeliever to continue to ignore the God who made them.

But for those with an open heart and open mind, the Bible indicates that the evidence for God is clear;

"For since the creation of the world God's invisible qualities —his eternal power and divine nature—have been clearly seen, being understood from what has been made, so that people are without excuse." (Romans 1:20).

At its heart, this evidence is easy to perceive and simple to understand. You do not need to read scientific journals and have a degree in genetics or cosmology to perceive it. The evidence is there for all to see. Look up at the stars at night or hold a new-born baby in your arms, and open your heart to the wonder of creation and the miracle of life. This universe is not an accident. It did not just come into being by itself. Life is an extraordinary miracle. The evidence is staring you in the face every day if you care to look!

THE VOICE OF CONSCIENCE

Our culpability is further extenuated by the conscience that God has created within each of us. The Bible indicates that God has placed a basic understanding of His standards of right and wrong within the human psyche, so that we are without excuse when we sin:

"The requirements of the law are written on their hearts, their consciences also bearing witness, and their thoughts some-

times accusing them and at other times even defending them." (Romans 2:15)

The existence of an innate, universal set of absolute moral values within the human conscience is strong evidence for the existence of God. Universally held, absolute moral standards cannot be explained bio-chemically, nor even socially. Ultimately, atheism, when it is extrapolated to its logical conclusion, requires the denial of absolute morality. If we are all simply animals who have crawled from the biological swamp, then there is no reason why I should be forced to conform to anyone else's standards of behaviour. Under this philosophy, each of us are free agents, unencumbered by ultimate accountability, and our individual behavioural and moral preferences are neither more nor less valid than anyone else's. I am not obligated to conform to any expectations or standards other than the pursuit of my own self-interest. This is because, ultimately, all morality is relative; just one person's opinion over another's.

Most atheists who understand the profound implications of their philosophy, concede this point: If God doesn't exist, then absolute moral values don't exist. Richard Dawkins, the noted atheist and evolutionary biologist, in his book *"The God Delusion"*, writes, *"Without God, there is no evil and no good: nothing but blind, pitiless indifference."*[22] Similarly, Fyodor Dostoevsky, the Russian novelist and philosopher, wrote, *"If there is no God, everything is permissible"*[23]. Jeremy Rifken, the American evolutionist, in his book, *"Algemy"*, wrote,

"We no longer believe ourselves to be guests in someone else's home and therefore obliged to make our behaviour conform to a set of pre-existing cosmic rules. It is our creation now; we make the rules, we establish the parameters, we create our own

world; and because we do, we no longer have to justify our behaviour. We are the architects of the universe, we are responsible to nothing outside ourselves, for we are the kingdom, the power and the glory forever and ever!"[24]

The problem with this philosophy is that objective moral values DO exist. Almost all people would agree that objective good and evil DO exist. Attributes such as love, justice and faithfulness are perceived as inherently good, while things such as murder, rape and child abuse are perceived as inherently evil. These objective values seem to be hard-wired into the human conscience, and those few individuals within our society who act against these values are rightly perceived by the rest of humanity as being flawed or sick. Michael Ruse, an atheistic philosopher, concedes the existence of objective good and evil when he says, *"The person who says it is morally acceptable to rape little children is just as mistaken as the person who says two plus two equals five."*[25]

The problem for atheism, is explaining how these universal, absolute moral values could have arisen from bio-chemical evolution. Some atheists attempt to argue that objective moral values arise as a result of social conditioning. While it is true that, for example, society tends to teach children these values, this does not necessarily negate that God is the ultimate source of those values. The fact that we learn these values from our parents and from society as a whole does not make them less true. In the same way, the fact that someone has to teach us mathematics does not mean that mathematics is not "true". Society's social conditioning is not some form of brainwashing; it arises from the fact that we, as a collective, have a strong, instinctive sense of absolute good and evil.

In attempting to explain the existence of universal morals

apart from God, the only argument left to atheists is that these standards have arisen from majority consensus, because society has deemed that certain behaviours accrue the greatest benefit for the collective whole in the long run. However, there is a fatal flaw in this argument. Establishing moral standards via majority vote does not guarantee their inherent goodness. The vast majority of Nazis in the second world war decided that it was a good idea to exterminate millions of Jews. The majority got it wrong! The fact that you and I perceive that act of attempted genocide to be inherently evil demonstrates that we are appealing to a higher moral standard; one that over-rides the populous majority vote. But what is that higher moral standard? Where did it come from? Atheism simply does not have an answer.

Many atheists find themselves in the awkward position of acknowledging the logical impossibility of absolutes if God does not exist, while simultaneously conceding that certain absolute moral standards *do* exist. Few atheists would disagree that the extermination of millions of Jews by the Nazi regime was anything other than evil in the absolute sense. Atheism has yet to offer a reasonable explanation for the existence of such absolutes.

The Christian response is that these absolute moral values have been stamped onto our consciences as part of being created in the image of God. The universal nature of these morals within humanity is evidence of the indelible stamp of God's image within our collective conscience. We have an innate sense of right and wrong, hard-wired into our psyche, so that we know, intrinsically, when we are sinning. The reason why sin is so often perpetrated under the cover of darkness and obfuscated by deliberate veils of secrecy is that, at a primal level, we are implicitly aware that our actions are wrong. This inherent sense of wrongness is the voice of our conscience, and it is this that renders us ultimately culpable. No one can claim ignorance of God's standards or that they were unaware of their wrong-doing.

NO EXCUSE

The Bible states, unequivocally, that non-culpable unbelief simply does not exist. The indictment of Romans 1:20 is that *"people are without excuse"*. The grandeur and complexity of creation proclaims the existence of an almighty Creator, and our consciences are infused with an innate awareness of His existence and His moral standards. Those who persistently suppress these truths may eventually convince themselves of God's non-existence, but they will still be held culpable.

Some of you reading this may regard yourselves as earnest seekers who have yet to be convinced of God's existence. You may claim that your current lack of belief is the result of insufficient convincing evidence, rather than wilful suppression of the truth. I have had conversations with many people in this position, and there is a question that is asked in almost every instance; *"If God exists, why doesn't He make Himself more obvious?"*. It is a valid question. Surely God wants people to know Him and be saved, so why does He make the evidence for His existence so subtle? If He truly doesn't want to send people to Hell, why doesn't He come out into the open so that we can all believe in Him? Why does He appear to be hiding?

These are important questions. God's apparent hiddenness is the topic of the next chapter.

Reflection Questions

1. What new insights have you gained from this chapter? Has this chapter changed any of your views?

2. What questions or challenges has this chapter raised for you?

3. Read Romans 1:18-20. In what ways do you think God's wrath is already "being revealed" against the wickedness of mankind?

4. How has God made His existence "plain" to us? (vv.19-20). See also Psalm 19:1-4.

5. If the Bible did not exist, what could we surmise about God by looking at creation?

6. If God's existence is so "plain to them", why do so many people disbelieve in Him?

7. Read Romans 2:15. What is this verse is saying?

8. Given that the Bible says that God has written His standards into our consciences, how might we explain the differences that exist within people's consciences? How do people end up with different moral standards?

9. How do the above verses refute the idea of non-culpable unbelief?

THREE

THE GOD WHO HIDES

If God wants people to believe in Him, why doesn't He just make Himself more obvious? Why does He appear to be hiding? Renowned atheist, Bertrand Russell (1872 – 1970), once stated, *"If I do come face to face with God when I die, I will demand an explanation as to why he made the evidence for his existence insufficient.*[1]*"* Carl Sagan (1934 – 1996), the noted cosmologist and atheist, similarly commented, *"Why doesn't God place a glowing cross in the night sky to serve as irrefutable proof of his existence?*[2]*"*.

Significantly, even the Bible concedes the elusive nature of God; *"If I go to the east, He is not there; if I go to the west, I do not find Him. When He is at work in the north, I do not see Him; when He turns to the south, I catch no glimpse of Him."*

(Job 23:8-9). Similarly, Isaiah states, *"Truly, you are a God who hides Himself"* (Isa 45:15). Isaiah is speaking not as a sceptic or an outsider; he was one of God's prophets. He enjoyed a special relationship with God. He heard from God from time to time, and God spoke through him to the nation. Yet even the great prophet Isaiah complains of God's elusiveness. It is the same complaint that many people make today; *"God, why are you so often silent and invisible? Why do you hide yourself from humanity? Why aren't you more obvious? It would save a whole lot of doubt and confusion if you just made yourself more obvious! Then a whole lot more people would believe in you and follow you! Isn't that what you want?!!"* In the words of Bruce Russell, in his review of Paul K. Moser's book, "The Elusive God; Reorienting Religious Epistemology"; *"Why doesn't God make his existence blazingly clear by some sort of heavenly fireworks, for those who have not responded to his subtle call?"*[3]

BEING MORE OBVIOUS WOULD HAVE MINIMAL IMPACT

The first part of the answer is that doing so would not be as effective as we might think. To those who ask God to reveal Himself in some sort of heavenly fireworks, I hasten to point out that He did precisely that on at least one occasion in history, to no avail. As God guided the Israelites throughout their desert wanderings, He manifested Himself in spectacular fashion:

"By day the Lord went ahead of them in a pillar of cloud to guide them on their way and by night in a pillar of fire to give them light, so that they could travel by day or night. Neither the

pillar of cloud by day nor the pillar of fire by night left its place in front of the people." (Exod 13:21-22)

This did not merely occur for a few days or weeks; God continued to manifest Himself in this way for a period of 40 years! So remarkable was this theophany (physical manifestation of God) that the surrounding nations all saw and heard of it, and were in awe of the God of the Jews:

"They have already heard that You, O LORD, are with these people and that You, O Lord, have been seen face to face, that Your cloud stays over them, and that You go before them in a pillar of cloud by day and a pillar of fire by night." (Num 14:14).

If you had asked any of the surrounding nations, or any of the Jews themselves, *"Does the God of the Jews exist?"* they would have responded, *"Of course He does! Just open your eyes and look! There He is!"* So amazing was this blazing manifestation of God, that Nehemiah was still talking about it hundreds of years later:

"By day You led them with a pillar of cloud, and by night with a pillar of fire to give them light on the way they were to take." (Neh 9:12)

So, what was the result of God's dramatic self-revelation? How did people respond to this physical, tangible, incontrovertible evidence of God in the world for 40 years? Surely it resulted in mass conversion? Surely the surrounding nations laid down their swords, repented and placed their faith in this great God whom they could see before their very eyes? No. The surrounding nations continued to oppose God and his people. They refused to repent and submit to God.

And the Jews themselves? Surely this indisputable physical sign strengthened their own faith and their resolve to follow

God? No. Shortly after the pillars of cloud and fire appeared, Moses went up Mount Sinai to receive the 10 commandments from God, and while he was gone someone said (and I paraphrase), *"Hey I've got a great idea! Let's make an idol and worship it!"* And everyone else said, *"Brilliant! Great idea! Let's do it!"*. And so that is what they did. With the awe inspiring, tangible presence of the true God right in front of their eyes, they turned their backs on Him, made a little golden calf, and started worshipping it. It's gob-smackingly stupid isn't it? It's almost too hard to believe that they could be that obtuse! And yet, that incident provides us with a window into the hardness of the human heart. Even when God shows up in front of us, incontrovertibly and spectacularly, we have a natural tendency to turn from Him towards idolatry and rebellion.

The truth is that God could do a lap of the earth in a fiery chariot every hour of every day, and most people would still not repent. All it would do would be to remove any doubts about His existence. When it became apparent that God was not immediately smiting people for their sins, life would resume as normal. People would go on having affairs, cheating on their tax returns, lying, stealing, being abusive, being greedy, living selfish lives, committing murder and rape and assault. God's irrefutable presence would be an intellectual curiosity that would not be allowed to interfere with the way we live our daily lives. That is what happened with the Israelites and the surrounding nations thousands of years ago, and it would happen again today – because mankind has not changed.

THE CONSEQUENCE OF THE FALL

One of the reasons why God is not visible to us, is because

of the Fall of mankind, recorded in Genesis 2 and 3. It is quite fascinating that Michelangelo's famous painting of the Fall, on the ceiling of the Sistine Chapel in Rome, has, over time, developed a stress fracture in the most remarkable of places, exactly separating the hand of man from the hand of God. This accident of degenerative plaster is a powerful metaphor depicting the enormous gulf that was created between the physical and spiritual realms when mankind rebelled against God in the beginning. In the words of the old saying, *"If God seems distant, guess who moved."*

The story of the Fall, in Genesis 3, is foundational for our understanding of the apparent hiddenness of God today. The first humans enjoyed a deeply personal relationship with God. They walked with Him and they talked with Him. Despite God's transcendent nature – His immensity, His incorporeal nature and His trans-dimensionality – He chose to appear in some visible form to Adam and Eve in the Garden of Eden. We are not told what form God took, but we must understand that this would have merely been a convenient theophany - a physical means of meaningfully interacting with His creation - rather than God limiting Himself to one physical location. All theophanies must be understood in this light. At the very moment when God may appear in some physical form, He is still fully and completely present at every point in the universe. A theophany does not cancel God's omnipresence. The point we need to underline here, however, is that in the very beginning – in the Garden of Eden – God was tangibly and visibly present with mankind.

The Fall, however, changed everything. A deep rift was created between us and God when we disobeyed Him. Mankind was expelled from the presence of God, and God's visible, tangible presence was withdrawn from the world. This has been our experience ever since. We cannot underestimate the impact of the Fall in creating distance between us and God. In essence, we told God that we did not want Him telling us what to do. We wanted to make our own decisions without His interference, and God has granted that wish by withdrawing His tangible presence. Mankind rejected God's right to dictate the terms of our lives – effectively telling Him to go away - and God has responded accordingly.

This explanation is, of course, entirely unsatisfactory to the average sceptic. *"You mean God isn't talking to me because of something someone else did thousands of years ago? He needs to get over it!"*

The lasting impact of the Fall, however, is only a small piece of the puzzle of God's apparent hiddenness. There are even deeper issues at play.

THE TRANSCENDENT NATURE OF GOD

A vital aspect to understanding the apparent hiddenness of God, is His transcendent nature. There are three aspects to God's transcendence that make Him seem elusive.

Firstly, the Bible says that *"God is spirit"* (Jn 4:24). In other words, He is incorporeal; He has no physical body. He is not a being of flesh and blood who can be seen and touched. On one occasion, at the end of a seminar where I had mentioned the incorporeal nature of God, a woman spoke up during question time, stating that *"everyone knows that God has a body that looks just like ours, because the Bible says that we were made in His image!"* When I asked her where she thought God was right now, she replied, *"In Heaven of course!"*. When I asked her where else He was, she began to falter as she started to see my point. God is everywhere; He is omnipresent, and that would not be possible if He had a physical body which was limited to one specific location. God is spirit, an entirely spiritual being, unbound by the restrictions of a physical body.

Secondly, God is immense. I don't mean this in terms of physical size, because, as a spiritual being, He is completely size-less. His immensity is one of pervasive presence rather than size, because God is everywhere. He is fully present at every point on planet earth. He is present in the deepest part of the ocean where no light ever reaches. He is present on the top of the world's highest mountains. He is present on the moons of Jupiter. He is present in the heart of the Andromeda Galaxy. He is fully present in the far flung reaches of the universe, billions of light years distant. God is everywhere! He is immense in His pervasive presence. Isaiah 48:13 says *"God holds the universe in the span of His hand"*, not to infer any inherent physicality in God's being, but simply to point out that, should He decide to manifest himself in a physical form, He could quite easily encapsulate the entire universe with its billions of galaxies within the palm of a single hand. Our lack of ability to perceive God clearly, and His apparent hiddenness, is, to some extent, a product of that immensity.

When I taught High School Christian Studies, I used to ask my students, *"Do you believe that something can be too big to see?"* I would often receive perplexed looks from many students. It is easy to conceptualise that something could be too small to see, but it is more difficult to conceive of something being too big to see. I would then proceed to give this illustration:

Imagine two sentient microbes, swimming around in my

bloodstream, who bump into each other and stop for a philosophical chat. They begin discussing whether Kevin Simington exists. After much debate, one says to the other, "*If he exists, where is he? Have any of the other microbes ever seen him? No! You show me Kevin Simington, and then I'll believe!*" The microbes have a major problem; I am too big for them to see. Yet, ironically, the whole time they are doubting my existence, they are actually living and moving and having their very existence within me. Acts 17:28 states, "*God is not far from any of us, for in Him we live and move and have our being*". The whole universe resides within the very essence of God! We live our lives within His being! Let me reiterate, this does not infer physicality on God's part. He is the immense spirit who easily encapsulates the entire universe. This is why He is not visible to us! The God who created the entire universe, with its billions of galaxies, and within whom that vast universe resides, is not going to be someone we will bump into at the local hotel or supermarket!

The third aspect of God's transcendence which makes Him appear elusive is His transdimensional nature. We live in a four-dimensional world; three physical dimensions plus time. The Bible indicates, however, that God is not bound by any of these dimensions. For example, God is timeless. You and I travel through time at the precise speed of one second per second. We cannot go forward any faster and we cannot go backwards at all. We are locked into the time continuum, perpetually stuck in the present. But God is present at every point in time simultaneously. He straddles time in the same way that we can straddle a ruler. He is present at the very beginning of creation and at the very end of human history, simultaneously. This is what is meant by God's description of

Himself; "*I am the Alpha and the Omega, the first and the last, the beginning and the end.*" (Rev 22:13). The eternal nature of God does not simply mean that He has lived forever in the past and will continue to exist forever into the future, travelling through time second by consecutive second. God exists at all times simultaneously. This is why God identified Himself to Moses as "*I am*" (Exodus 3:14). Moses asked God what His name is, and God replied; "*I am who I am,*" adding, "*Say this to the people of Israel, 'I am' has sent me to you.*" God's use of the word "*I am*" ('Ehye [אֶהְיֶה]) as a name for Himself, introduces the mind-bending concept that God exists in the eternal present at every point in time. In one sense, there is no past or future for God, because He exists at every point in time simultaneously. This is why some predictive prophecies in the Bible are written in the present tense, because, from God's perspective, they are the present. Time is a construct that God has created for the physical universe, but He is not limited by it. (Various philosophical attempts to explain this - omnitemporalism, metatemporalism, atemporalism and sempiternalism - are beyond the scope of this book, but further reading in those areas may assist in alleviating insomnia!)

Time is just one example of God's trans-dimensionality. In His book, "*Beyond The Cosmos*",[4] Christian scientist, Dr. Hugh Ross, points to the mounting scientific speculation within the field of cosmology, together with certain mathematical extrapolations from string theory, indicating the existence of multiple dimensions beyond our four-dimensional universe. He examines hints within the Bible of God's multi-dimensionality, including the reference in Genesis 1 and Hebrews 11 of God creating the "*visible from the invisible*".

While this level of philosophical speculation is beyond our

current purposes, we can, at the very least, recognise that the Bible indicates that God exists beyond the normal dimensions of space and time, because He created these. He is transdimensional, and we simply cannot expect to perceive such a being in any meaningful way, from our limited perspective. God's apparent hiddenness is partly a direct corollary of His transdimensional nature.

THE INCARNATION OF CHRIST

Given the transcendent, transdimensional nature of God, it is surprising that we are able to perceive Him in any way at all. The fact that we can, however, arises from God's deliberate revelation of Himself to us. We have already discussed His revelation through the natural world and through conscience, and Christians believe that the Bible is another means by which God has disclosed aspects of Himself to mankind. By far the most profound self-revelation of God to mankind, however, is the incarnation of Christ. The Apostle John writes, *"The Word became flesh and made His dwelling among us. We have seen His glory, the glory of the one and only Son, who came from the Father, full of grace and truth"* (John 1:14). Over 2,000 years ago, God injected Himself into human history, taking on the form and nature of a human being, in order to interact and communicate with us at our limited level. This is hardly the action of a God who is hiding from us! Of course, for those of us living in the 21st century, we missed it, but if we had been born in the early decades of 1st century Palestine, we could have seen and heard God in the flesh.

The incarnation of Christ is God's ultimate message to mankind. It is a message delivered personally, in the flesh, in the form of Jesus Christ, who lived among us for 33 years. For sceptics who doubt the existence of God and who accuse Him of not revealing Himself, the life, death and resurrection of Jesus Christ offers a profound answer. God once visited our planet personally, and the evidence of that visit is overwhelming.

I am occasionally amazed to meet someone who believes that Jesus never existed. This is an absurd position to hold that completely overlooks the considerable weight of historical evidence. In my experience, the only people who hold this view are those who have no historical training and have not bothered to examine the evidence. The life of Christ is substantiated by a number of extra-biblical writers from antiquity, including Cornellius Tacitus, Lucian, Flavius Josephus, Suetonius, Pliny the Younger, Thallus, Philegon and Mara Bar-Serapion. Respected historian, Neil Carter, who is a professed atheist, writes:

"I can't believe I'm feeling the need to do this, but today I'd like to write a brief defence of the historicity of Jesus. When people in the sceptic community argue that Jesus never existed, they are dismissing a large body of work for which they have insufficient appreciation, most often due to the fact that they themselves have never formally studied the subject.... The earliest writings which attest to the existence of Jesus come from the apostle Paul, a leather worker by day and preacher by night ... sometime in the mid-50s AD... The oral tradition which later came to inform the writing of the gospels predates the ministry of Paul by many years... Paul didn't invent these stories..."[5]

Dr. Bart Ehrman is a respected historian who is a professed agnostic. He was recently interviewed by "The Atheist Guy" on "Atheist Radio" (an internet radio station whose sole aim is to discredit Christianity)⁶. Here is a transcript of part of that interview:

Atheist Guy: *Do you believe that Jesus actually existed?*

Dr. Ehrman: *Yes. There is no serious historian who doubts the existence of Jesus. There are a lot of people who want to write sensational books claiming that Jesus didn't exist, but I don't know any serious scholar who doubts the existence of Jesus.*

Atheist Guy: *But there are historians who disagree with you, aren't there?*

Dr. Ehrman: *None that I've ever heard of. Not serious historians. I know thousands of scholars of the ancient world and I don't know any one of these scholars who disagree.*

Of course, it is one thing to concede that Jesus existed, it is quite another to accept the accounts of His miracles. Yet, even in these details, there is extra-biblical corroboration. The Talmud, one of the sacred texts of Judaism that was being written at the time of Christ, mentions the miracles of Jesus on 14 separate occasions. The Jewish rabbis could not deny His miracles, because they had been witnessed by, in some instances, thousands of people! Instead, they attributed them to the power of the devil. It defies belief how anyone could possibly believe that the devil would be interested in healing the blind, healing the sick, raising up quadriplegics, feeding the hungry and raising people from the dead! Ultimately, the Jews could not silence Jesus nor staunch the constant flow of miracles, so they executed Him for claiming to be God. One has to ask what further verification they would require of One who claimed to be God, other than the extraordinary, supernatural miracles of Jesus. The important point for our consideration here, however, is that even Jesus' enemies could not deny His miracles, and even wrote about them in their sacred text!

The greatest proof of Jesus' claim to be God was, of course, His resurrection from the dead. If His claim of divinity had had no substance, if it arose from mental delusion or deliberate fraud, the grave would have been the end of the matter, refuting His claims conclusively. But the Bible records Jesus' resurrection from the dead. According to the Gospel accounts, Jesus rose to life and appeared to His followers over a period of 40 days, with Paul mentioning one occasion when he appeared to a crowd of over 500 people (1 Cor 15:1-11).

Not only do we have the Biblical accounts of the resurrection, but the ancient Jewish writer, Flavius Josephus, also mentions Jesus' resurrection, in his book, *"The Antiquities Of The Jews"*.[7]

Those who claim that God is hiding from us, and that He has not given us enough evidence of His existence, are ignoring the most extraordinary evidence of all; the resurrection of Jesus Christ from the dead. If the accounts of the miracles and resurrection of Jesus are true, then we have incontrovertible evidence of the existence of God. Realising this, several academics and historians have, over the years, set out to disprove the resurrection story. Their philosophy was simple; disprove the resurrection and you remove the strongest argument for the existence of God. Not only have these attempts been unsuccessful, they have regularly led to the complete capitulation and conversion of those undertaking the research:

- **Sir William Mitchell Ramsay** (1851-1939)

was a highly respected historian and archaeologist from Scotland. He set out to prove the historical inaccuracies of Luke and Acts. He spent 15 years researching and digging, only to end up being convinced of the incredible accuracy of the New Testament. He converted to Christianity, and called Luke one of the greatest historians to ever live. He wrote several books on the subject, which have stood the test of time. His work caused an outcry from atheists because they had been funding his research and were eagerly awaiting his results in disproving the validity of the New Testament.[8]

- **Albert Henry Ross** (1881-1950) was an English journalist and author who set out to disprove the myth of the resurrection. He was planning on writing a paper called *"Jesus – The Last Phase"*, but he became converted during the course of his investigations. He wrote the classic book *"Who Moved The Stone?"*[9] under the pseudonym Frank Morison. The book has led many people to faith in Christ.

- **Lee Strobel** was a journalist for the Chicago Tribune. His wife converted to Christianity and Lee became very concerned. In order to "rescue" his wife from the church, he set out to disprove Christianity, focussing on the resurrection story. He spent 18 months, utilising his skills as a researcher and investigative reporter, interviewing experts from around the world, and studying the 1st century documents for himself. The overwhelming evidence for the resurrection of Christ eventually led to his own conversion, and he went on to write the now famous book, *"The Case For Christ"*[10] (recently made into a movie), along with several other books in the series, which have led many people to faith in Christ.

The incarnation of Christ is a complete repudiation of the claim that God is hiding from us! While we may wish God to be as obvious to us today as He was in the life of Jesus, we simply cannot ignore the fact that, at one point in history, God spoke to humanity not with a whisper, but with a megaphone. The life, death and resurrection of His Son, Jesus Christ, is extremely compelling evidence for God's existence, and provides us with a stunning insight into His character and nature.

THE NECESSITY OF FAITH

Apart from God's unequivocal revelation through the life of Jesus, His disclosure of Himself to mankind on an ongoing basis remains subtle. While the Bible indicates that the evidence for God's existence within nature and conscience are sufficient for those who are earnestly seeking, one could hardly accuse God of overplaying His hand. Hence the complaint of both Isaiah and Job, echoed by countless people today, regarding God's apparent hiddenness. So, the question remains, why doesn't God make Himself more obvious?

The Bible's answer is that God desires faith in those who will follow Him. The well-known encounter between Jesus and "doubting Thomas" illustrates this. In Jesus' first post-resurrection appearance to the disciples as a group, Thomas was absent. When the disciples subsequently told Thomas the amazing news that they had seen Jesus alive, he did not believe them, stating, *"Unless I see the nail marks in His hands and put my fingers where the nails were, and put my hand into His side, I will not believe."* (John 20:25). Thomas was demanding undeniable proof before he would believe, in the same way that people continue to demand it today. The conclusion to the story is worth reading in full:

"A week later his disciples were in the house again, and Thomas was with them. Though the doors were locked, Jesus came and stood among them and said, "Peace be with you!" Then He said to Thomas, "Put your finger here; see my hands. Reach out your hand and put it into my side. Stop doubting and believe." Thomas said to Him, "My Lord and my God!" Then Jesus told him, "Because you have seen me, you have believed; blessed are those who have not seen and yet have believed." (John 20:26-29)

The concluding words of Jesus in that encounter are significant; *"blessed are those who have not seen and yet have believed"*. In other words, God desires His followers to exhibit faith, without the luxury of final and unequivocal proof. He does not want to overwhelm our senses to the point where we have no choice but to believe. In Hebrews 11:1 we read, *"Now faith is confidence in what we hope for and assurance about what we do not see."* It is the fact that *"we do not see"*, yet still choose to believe that makes faith so honourable in God's eyes. The essential nature of this kind of faith is further explained a few verses later; *"Without faith it is impossible to please God, because anyone who comes to Him must believe that He exists and that He rewards those who earnestly seek Him."* (Heb 11:6). God is looking for people who will believe in Him without the necessity of final proof. Without this kind of unproven faith, it is *"impossible to please God."*

I have had several conversations with sceptics regarding God's insistence upon unproven faith, and their usual response goes something like this; *"Why does God demand this kind of blind faith? We don't treat our own children like this. We don't hide ourselves from them, yet their love for us is not diminished by the fact that they can see us."* There are several things to say in response.

Firstly, there is a difference between blind faith and unproven faith. Blind faith is belief based upon a complete lack of evidence. Unproven faith, on the other hand, is based upon evidence which is substantial and convincing, yet which stops short of ultimate proof. In the case of God's existence there **is** substantial and convincing evidence.

Secondly, God's insistence of faith in His followers arises partly from His desire to not overwhelm them to the point where they have no choice but to believe. Free choice is extremely important in God's eyes.

Thirdly, God also realises that, for many people, no amount of evidence will be ever be enough. An incident in the life of Jesus illustrates this. In Matthew 12:38, some religious leaders confronted Jesus and demanded, *"If you are from God, give us a sign from heaven."* The extraordinary thing about their demand was that prior to this, Jesus had healed the sick, raised the dead, walked on water, turned water into wine, multiplied food to feed thousands of people and calmed a storm with the command of His voice! What more did they expect? How could they not be convinced already? For these miracles were undeniable, having been witnessed, on some occasions, by thousands of people.

Jesus' response to the request of these religious leaders for a further sign was scathing; *"A wicked and adulterous generation looks for a miraculous sign, but none will be given them except the sign of Jonah."* (Matt 12:39). Jesus condemned their hardness of heart, calling their unbelief in the face of such convincing evidence *"wicked and adulterous."* The *"sign of Jonah"* is a prophetic reference to His impending death and resurrection. Just as Jonah was in the belly of the fish for three days until re-emerging unharmed and whole into the world, so, too, He would be in the grave for three days before rising again. Jesus was saying that if these hard-hearted leaders would not believe the evidence of the miracles He was performing, the only sign remaining for them would be His resurrection from the dead. Jesus' response to those critics is God's response to sceptics today; the death and resurrection of Jesus is a sufficient sign for those who are earnestly seeking God, and no sign will ever be enough for those who aren't.

Reflection Questions

1. *What new insights have you gained from this chapter? Has this chapter changed any of your views?*

2. *What questions or challenges has this chapter raised for you?*

3. *Read Exodus 13:21-22. Given the spectacular nature of this theophany, how can we explain the extraordinary idolatry of Israel shortly afterwards, when they made a golden calf and started worshipping it? (Exodus 32). What does this say about human nature?*

4. Read Genesis 3. How does this chapter help to explain the apparent hiddenness of God?

5. Read John 4:24. What is your understanding of the nature of God in regard to this? Does God have a body? If not, how do we explain the fact that God was "walking in the garden" with Adam and Eve in Genesis 2:8?

6. Read Acts 17:28. What does this say about the relationship between God and the physical universe? How does it help explain the apparent hiddenness of God?

7. Read John 1:1-18. How does this passage provide an answer to those who accuse God of hiding? What does it mean to say that Jesus was fully human and fully God?

8. Read Hebrews 11:6. There is no doubt that God could make Himself more obvious than He currently does. This verse, however, explains why He doesn't. What is the reason and why?

9. Read Matthew 12:38-39. Why does God refuse to prove Himself unequivocally to mankind?

FOUR

THE GOD WHO WANTS TO BE FOUND

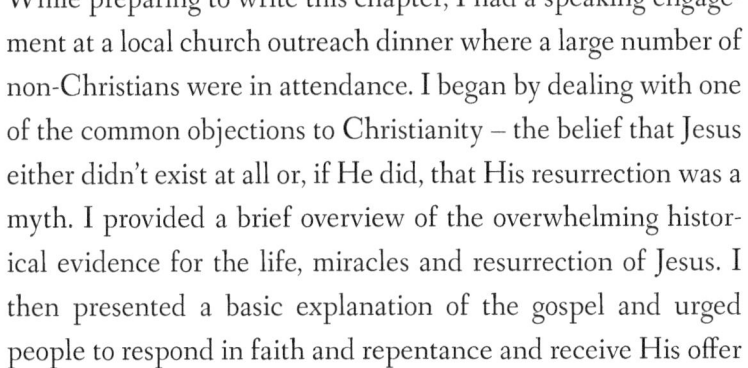

While preparing to write this chapter, I had a speaking engagement at a local church outreach dinner where a large number of non-Christians were in attendance. I began by dealing with one of the common objections to Christianity – the belief that Jesus either didn't exist at all or, if He did, that His resurrection was a myth. I provided a brief overview of the overwhelming historical evidence for the life, miracles and resurrection of Jesus. I then presented a basic explanation of the gospel and urged people to respond in faith and repentance and receive His offer of forgiveness. I concluded with an exhortation to seek God with all their heart, quoting from Jeremiah 29:13, *"You will seek me and find me, when you seek me with all your heart."*

After my talk I was approached by a Christian man in his

late 50's, called Ron, who shared the story of how he had sought and found God when he was in his 20's. He had been a member of an outlaw biker gang and had been living a wild life. He recounted stories of some of the terrible things he had done, and how dark and violent his heart had been. On one of his many drunken bike rides he had a horrendous crash and was in a coma for 3 days, yet even such a serious incident did not cause him to stop and evaluate the path he was on. Eventually his life of crime and violence caught up with him. He was arrested, charged and convicted for armed robbery and attempted murder. He was sentenced to 7 years in prison and was sent to the maximum-security section of one of Australia's largest prisons.

At this point in the story he simply said to me, "*That's where I found the Lord*". I asked him, "*How did that happen?*". In my mind's eye, I pictured him being befriended by the prison chaplain, starting to attend church services, asking lots of questions, beginning to read the Bible and gradually developing a faith that ultimately blossomed into a genuine commitment to Christ as Lord and Saviour. I was wrong! I'll let Ron tell you how it really happened in his own words;

"*It was my second night in prison. I was alone in my cell and I was absolutely terrified. I was facing seven years in a maximum-security prison and I knew I couldn't do it. I remember thinking, 'I'm not gonna make it.' I was in a really bad way. I realised what a mess I'd made of my life and I felt like I was at the bottom of a deep black hole with no way out. I fell to my knees on the concrete floor and I raised my arms to heaven and I cried out to God with all my heart. My prayer went something like this; 'God I don't know whether you're there or not, but if you are, please help me! I can't do this on my own! Please help me! Please come into my life! Please rescue me! I need you! I'm sorry for what I've done. Please help me!' Immediately God turned up in a big way. I physically felt Him wrap His arms around me and I was completely overwhelmed by a feeling of warmth and love and joy – like nothing I had ever experienced before in my life. The feeling of God's presence coursed through my body from head to foot. I started thanking and praising Him, and I was so overwhelmed by His presence that I was sobbing uncontrollably from sheer joy."*

Wow! Ron has been a Christian now for over 30 years. After prison he married a wonderful Christian lady and worked as a youth minister, then as a counsellor in a drug rehabilitation facility. He is now retired and if you were to meet him you would have a strong impression of someone who has walked closely with the Lord for many years. In fact, as I spoke with him, I couldn't help wondering why the church hadn't asked him to do the outreach talk instead of me!

THE PROMISE OF DISCLOSURE

Ron's story illustrates an important truth; God is ready and willing to respond to people who genuinely reach out to Him in humility and repentance. God may appear to be hiding, but He is not hiding very well. He wants to be found. The promise of Jeremiah 29:13 is genuine;

"You will seek me and find me, when you seek me with all your heart"

This is an absolute guarantee. God wants to be found, and He promises us that He will reveal himself to us if we earnestly seek Him. Significantly, we are not exhorted to seek God with all our mind, but with all our heart. What characterised Ron's encounter with God was the whole-hearted nature of his cry for help. He was not demanding that God prove himself by answering a list of intellectual objections; he was simply crying out for mercy and begging God to help him. There is a profound difference between saying *"God, I need you to prove yourself to me"* and *"God I need you"*. The former makes God your servant, the latter places you on your knees, where you belong!

Over the years I have met many people who claim that they have prayed *"God, if you're there, show yourself to me – prove to me that you exist"*, but have had no response. These people will often say something to me like, "I gave God a chance to prove Himself, but He never showed up, therefore He doesn't exist". What they fail to realise, however, is how arrogant this approach to God is. In doing this, they appoint themselves as judge. They place God in the dock, accusing Him of non-existence, demanding that He show up and prove Himself to their own satisfaction. Often, when I speak with people such as this, I get the impression that they were already operating from a position of extreme scepticism, and were effectively daring God to show up and prove them wrong.

This is a far cry from seeking God with *"all your heart"* (Jer 29:13). The transcendent, trans-dimensional, all-powerful, eternal Creator of the universe is not going to come scampering in response to the arrogant demands of sceptics and perform a cute magic trick to satisfy them. He is not a performer in our play. He is not a defendant in our courtroom. Nor is He a servant to be ordered around. There is a profound arrogance in the attitude that effectively says, *"I will only believe in God if I can have all my objections resolved and all my questions answered. God must prove himself to me before I will have faith in Him.*" God's response to people who treat Him in this condescending manner is articulated in James 4:6, *"God opposes the proud, but gives grace to the humble".* God simply refuses to play ball with those who demand that He reveal Himself on their terms. On the other hand, He responds with grace to those who approach Him humbly and whole-heartedly. Psalm 34:18 states, *"The Lord is close to the brokenhearted and saves those who are crushed in spirit."* Ron's brokenhearted cry for help from his lonely prison cell epitomises the way we must all approach God – humbly recognising our weakness and sin, and asking for God's mercy.

The promise of Jeremiah 29:13, (*"You will seek me and find me, when you seek me with all your heart"*), is not a promise to have all our questions answered and all our objections resolved. It is not a promise to have everything explained to our satisfaction. It is not a promise to grant us complete enlightenment so that we may finally understand the complexities of the universe's philosophical conundrums. It is simply a promise that we will "***find***" God when we "*seek Him with all our heart*" (Jer 29:13). It is a promise that we will encounter God experientially.

It is vital that we understand the exact nature of God's promise of disclosure at this point. God is not promising that we will understand Him (at least not fully), but that we will experience Him, in a profound, personal way. The promise of a personal encounter is reflected in Psalm 34:8, *"Taste and see that the Lord is good".* This is not inviting us to mere intellectual assent, but to tangibly encounter God.

A pivotal event in the life of the late Billy Graham serves to illustrate this truth. In 1949, Billy Graham, only 30 years old, was preparing for a crusade in Los Angeles. He was unaware that this would be the crusade that would launch him to international fame and influence, opening the door for him to ultimately preach the gospel to millions of people over the course of his life. But as he prepared, he was plagued with doubts; not concerning the existence of God or the divinity of Christ, but about the reliability of the Bible. His friend, Charles Templeton had become a liberal, and had been sowing seeds of doubt in Billy Graham's mind. He posed serious questions about the Bible's veracity, pointing to supposed transmission errors, interpolations and contradictions. Billy Graham had no answers to Templeton's accusations and became increasingly confused and unsure. He reached a crisis point where he felt that he could not preach if he continued to have these doubts. The Los Angeles crusade – and the rest of his future ministry – was hanging in the balance. Finally, things came to a climax when Graham went for a walk one night in the San Bernadino mountains. He fell to his knees and cried out to God for help. He confessed that he didn't have all the answers to the intellectual questions posed by Templeton. Writing about this moment in his biography, Graham records his prayer, *"Father, I am going to accept this Bible as Thy Word, by faith! I'm going to allow faith to go beyond my intellectual questions and doubts, and I will believe this to be Your inspired Word."* As he rose from his knees, Graham says that he felt overwhelmed by the presence of God, a tangible sense of the power and enveloping immediacy of God that was undeniable, and which moved him to tears. His questions were still unanswered, but his previous doubts had been completely swept away by God's tangible, powerful, enveloping presence.[1]

Psalm 46:10 says, *"Be still and know that I am God."* In other words, God sometimes asks us to put aside our frantic striving, our desperate need to work everything out, our need to resolve every aspect of a problem, and simply rest in the stillness of His presence. It is this personal encounter of God's tangible presence that is at the heart of Christian confidence and faith. Christianity is not a religion of blind faith, but one in which adherents have their faith overwhelmingly confirmed by the self-authenticating witness of God's Spirit within them. In Romans 8:15-16, Paul writes, *"For you did not receive a spirit that makes you a slave again to fear, but you received the Spirit of sonship. And by Him you cry, 'Abba, Father'. The Spirit Himself testifies with our spirit that we are God's children."* It is this internal experience of God's Spirit, the interaction of God's Spirit with our own spirit, that enables the Christian to experience unshakeable faith despite not having all the answers.

This is not to diminish the value of intellectual, evidence-based enquiry. Christianity certainly does not require that we undertake a spiritual lobotomy in order to believe. There are plenty of highly qualified academics, at the top of their chosen fields, who have investigated the central tenets of Christianity and have discovered a faith that is reasonable and rational. Yet the Bible demands that, at some point in our search for God, we must move beyond the intellectual level, to a quest that involves *"all your heart"* (Jer 29:13). God does not wish to be an object of mere intellectual curiosity; He desires to engage with us intimately and personally.

THE GOD OF RELATIONSHIP

God calls us into relationship with Him; the restoration of a relationship that was broken in the Fall at the beginning of human history. The language of relationship permeates the Bible's description of knowing God:

- *"fellowship with God"* (1 John 1:3)
- *"walking with God"* or God *"walking"* with us (Genesis 5:22-24; 6:9; Lev 26:12; 2 Cor 6:16)
- *"dwelling"* with God (Exod 33:14-17; Zech 2:10; 2 Cor 6:16)
- *"living"* or *"abiding"* with God (John 14:23; John 17:21-23; 1 John 3:24)
- *"friendship"* with God (Gen 18:1-8)

Ultimately, Christianity is not a religion of cold belief; it is a friendship with God that is experiential and transformative. This is a truly radical concept, unique in all the world's religions. The God of the universe wishes us to encounter Him at a profoundly personal level. And it is to people who earnestly seek such a transformative encounter that God promises to reveal Himself personally.

I have encountered people who have struggled for years to believe in God. They have wrestled with doubts, struggled with intellectual objections and posed questions for which they have not found satisfying, rational answers. I have witnessed their frustration as they have sincerely sought to understand God. But that is precisely their problem! Their search for God is a search of the mind, not a search of the heart. They are seeking to know <u>about</u> God, instead of seeking to <u>know</u> God. They are attempting to understand God instead of opening their hearts to encounter God. The truth is that none of us will ever fully understand God on this side of eternity. We will never reach the point where all our questions are answered and we perceive the spiritual realm with perfect clarity. If I insist that I must understand someone completely before I believe in them, then I would not believe in my wife! In human relationships we choose to relate to others without fully understanding them. This is even more necessary in regard to God. We are imperfect, three-dimensional beings attempting to understand a transcendent, infinite, trans-dimensional God!

Many Christians testify that intellectual enquiry only took them so far in their journey towards faith; that they reached a point where they could go no further with rational investigation and needed to take a step of faith. What does that mean? What does *"taking a step of faith"* look like? In essence it means opening your heart to God and asking that He would meet you and encounter you at a personal rather than an intellectual level. *"You will seek me and find me, when you seek me with all your heart."* (Jer 29:13). This will involve leaving aside your unanswered questions and choosing to open yourself to God despite your incomplete understanding. Necessarily, it will involve the twin elements of repentance and faith. We must turn from something and turn to something. We turn from our rebellion, asking for forgiveness, and pledging to live to honour God now. We turn to Christ, trusting in His death and resurrection for our forgiveness, and opening our hearts to receive Him as Lord. For those who genuinely take this step of faith, seeking God with all their heart, God promises to be found. The Bible promises, *"Draw near to God, and He will draw near to you."* (James 4:8).

In the end, it is the search of the heart that will lead people to God. And it is the subsequent experience of God that will answer their doubts. I do not doubt God's existence, not because I have obtained answers to all my questions, but because I have encountered God in an undeniable way since opening my heart to Him. And, in so doing, I discovered, as millions of other Christians have discovered, that *"God is not far from any of us, for in Him we live and move and have our being"* (Acts 17:28).

Reflection Questions

1. What new insights have you gained from this chapter? Has this chapter changed any of your views?

2. What questions or challenges has this chapter raised for you?

3. Read Jeremiah 29:13. What is the promise of this verse?

4. A key phrase in Jeremiah 29:13 is "with all your heart". What does this mean and why is it important? How is it different from the way many sceptics approach their "search" for God?

5. What does the Jeremiah 29:13 reveal about the character of God?

6. How should we respond to people who claim that they have earnestly searched for God but have not found Him?

7. Read 2 Corinthians 4:3-4. How does this help explain the ongoing unbelief of some people? How should this impact our efforts to evangelise?

8. Read Romans 8:15-16. What role does the Holy Spirit play in our ability to find and encounter God?

9. Read Acts 17:28. How far is God from any of us? How should this impact our attitude to evangelism?

FIVE

THE HISTORICITY OF JESUS AND THE BIBLE

The life, death and resurrection of Jesus Christ provides the strongest possible evidence for the existence of God. If the Biblical accounts of the events of His life are historically accurate, then the question, *"Does God exist?"* has been answered in the most emphatic, unequivocal way. Of course, this begs the question, *"Is the Biblical account of Jesus' life accurate? Does it reflect actual history or is it merely a fanciful embellishment of an ancient mythological figure?"* Whole books have been written addressing this issue, defending the historicity of Christ and the reliability of the Bible. In this chapter I will summarise some of the central arguments proposed by apologists and historians.

. . .

THE HISTORICITY OF JESUS

Atheists and sceptics, recognising the centrality of the life of Christ to the Christian message, have focused a significant amount of effort, over many years, in seeking to discredit the historicity of the life of Jesus. Their attacks have fallen into two categories; attempting to prove that Jesus never existed, and attempting to prove that his life was significantly embellished by the writers of the Bible. Let us examine these two attacks:

The Claim That Jesus Never Existed

I have already dealt with this claim, briefly, in Chapter 3, where I pointed out that only those with no historical training attempt to use this argument, because the historical evidence for the existence of Jesus is overwhelming. Leaving aside the Biblical accounts themselves, there is a significant additional corroboration for the life of Jesus Christ. The life of Christ is substantiated by a number of extra-biblical writers from antiquity, including Cornellius Tacitus, Lucian, Flavius Josephus, Suetonius, Pliny the Younger, Thallus, Philegon and Mara Bar-Serapion. As previously quoted (in Chapter 3), respected historian, Neil Carter, who is a professed atheist, writes:

"I can't believe I'm feeling the need to do this, but today I'd like to write a brief defence of the historicity of Jesus. When people in the sceptic community argue that Jesus never existed, they are dismissing a large body of work for which they have insufficient appreciation, most often due to the fact that they themselves have never formally studied the subject."[1]

Also previously quoted, respected historian and professed agnostic, Dr. Bart Ehrman, when interviewed on "Atheist Radio" on December 30th, 2011, stated, *"There is no serious historian who doubts the existence of Jesus. There are a lot of people who want to write sensational books claiming that Jesus didn't exist, but I don't know any serious scholar who doubts the existence of Jesus."*[2]

The Claim That Jesus' Life Was Significantly Embellished

Recognising the hopelessness of trying disprove Jesus' existence, the major thrust of the atheistic attack upon Jesus has been the attempt to discredit the veracity of the Biblical accounts of His life. Sceptics argue that Jesus' life was significantly embellished by the New Testament writers in order to promulgate a new religion – a religion which His followers had invented. According to this theory, Jesus was just an ordinary man who said a few wise things and developed a popular following. After His death, His followers deified Him (declared Him to be God), concocting stories of supposed miracles and fabricating the myth of His resurrection. The problem with this theory is that it is refuted by the Criteria of Historical Reliability.

The Criteria of Historical Reliability

In assessing whether an ancient document is historically reliable, historians apply multiple tests. These tests are commonly referred to as Criteria of Historical Reliability. The most commonly employed criteria are as follows:

- The Criterion of Time Gap
- The Criterion of Embarrassment

- The Criterion of Multiple Attestation
- The Criterion of The Absence of Protestation
- The Criterion of Corroboration by Hostile Critics
- The Criterion of Author Credibility

Space does not permit a full explanation of each of these, but a brief overview of the criteria will help you to understand why the New Testament letters, and the Gospels in particular, are widely regarded as historical documents of the highest calibre.

The Criteria of Time Gap and The Absence of Protestation (Criteria 1 and 4)

In historical terms, "time gap" refers to the amount of elapsed time between the actual historical events and the time of writing (when those events were eventually written down). In order for successful embellishment to occur, a significant amount of time has to elapse, so that there are very few, if any, eye-witnesses left alive who could refute the embellishment.

Professor A. N. Sherwin-White (1911-1993) was a world renowned Greco-Roman historian who, among his many scholarly works, analysed ancient historical embellishments. He concluded that minor embellishment required a time gap of at least two generations, while major embellishment required at least 200 years.[3] In other words, even minor mythological embellishment can't gain traction if it is written within the lifespan of the first two generations after the event, because there are too many people still alive who know the facts and who could speak up and refute the embellishment.

Let me give you an example. At the time of this book's

publication, it is 73 years since Winston Churchill led the Allies to victory over Adolf Hitler and the Nazis. Suppose I decided to write a biography of Churchill and I concocted all kinds of fanciful stories of him working miracles, raising people from the dead, walking on water and rising from the dead himself. I would very quickly be shut down as a fool and my written account would be overwhelmed by a flood of literary rebuttal. And in 2,000 years time, anyone investigating my ridiculous claims would uncover a veritable sea of indignant refutation. Even after more than 70 years have elapsed, I still could not get away with embellishing the life of Winston Churchill!

In the case of the life of Jesus Christ, the first three Gospels (Matthew, Mark and Luke) were written only 30-35 years after Jesus' death, and the Gospel of John was written another 25 years later. In other words, the Gospels were written within the lifetime of the eye-witnesses to the events of Jesus' life. And the response of the ancient world to those Gospels was remarkable; the Gospels were met with RESOUNDING SILENCE. No refutation. No protest. The reason for this is quite simple. No one could refute the Gospels because there were still thousands of eye witnesses alive who had witnessed Jesus' miracles. Hundreds had witnessed Him raise people from the dead. Thousands had witnessed Him heal the sick, the blind, the paralysed. Thousands had witnessed Him multiply food in order to feed the hungry. Even Jesus' resurrection from the dead was witnessed by hundreds. The Apostle Paul, in 1 Corinthians 15:6, tells us that on one occasion Jesus appeared alive again to a crowd of more than 500 people. As the Gospels were written and distributed in first century Palestine, there were literally thousands of eye witnesses who could verify their veracity. That is why we do not find any literary refutation in the historical record. If the Gospel accounts were fanciful embellishments by some deluded followers, we would expect to find a flood of literary refutation. But there is none.

Significantly, if the resurrection of Jesus was a myth, foisted upon the world by His over-zealous disciples, the Jewish authorities could have easily quashed the rumours by producing the dead body of Jesus. The fact that they did not do so is significant. In fact, the absence of protestation by the authorities is astounding. Not only did they fail to produce a dead body, but they also failed to write a single word refuting either the resurrection of Jesus' or His miracles. Because they couldn't! The facts were simply irrefutable; Jerusalem and the whole of Judea and Galilee were full of eye witnesses who could verify the events.

Both the extremely short time gap and the complete absence of protestation are two vital criteria in establishing the historical veracity of the Gospel accounts of the life of Jesus.

The Criterion Of Embarrassment (Criterion 2)

The criterion of embarrassment is a means of assessing the likelihood of authenticity and accuracy in a historical account. If an account contains content that is somewhat embarrassing to its author, it is presumed to be true, as the author would have no reason to invent an account which might embarrass him or her. In terms of the New Testament documents, there are several occurrences of "embarrassing" revelations that lend credibility to the probable veracity of the texts. These include:

- Peter's denial of Christ (which paints Peter in a bad

light)
- The crucifixion of Jesus, which was regarded as the most shameful way to die. People inventing a religion would not fabricate such a story of the death of their leader.
- The disbelief of Thomas (which paints another Apostle in a bad light)
- Jesus' close association with outcasts, prostitutes and sinners
- The healing of the blind man in Mark 8:22-26 where the first attempt is not completely successful.

The Criterion of Multiple Attestation (Criterion 3)

This test simply means that the more independent sources that report the same event, the more likely that event is to be historically accurate. In the case of the Biblical account of the life of Jesus, there is both internal and external multiple attestation. In terms of internal multiple attestation, many of the events of Jesus' life were recorded by multiple writers within the Bible itself: Matthew, Mark, Luke, John, James, Peter, Paul, John the elder and Jude. This is not to be undervalued, for these writers wrote from geographic and temporal isolation and their unified voice is particularly impressive. In terms of external multiple attestation, a number of events in the life of Jesus are corroborated by external sources:

- **Cornelius Tacitus**, a Roman senator, described the death of Jesus at the hands of Pilate[4]

- **Gaius Suetonius Tranquillus**, a Roman Historian, referred to Christ as the leader of the sect of Christians that was plaguing Rome.[5]
- **Thallus**, a first century Greek / Roman historian, described the supernatural darkness and the earthquakes that accompanied the crucifixion of Christ (recorded in all three synoptic Gospels – Matthew, Mark and Luke). His reference is quoted in the early second century by the historian, Africanus; *"On the whole world there pressed a fearful darkness, and the rocks were rent by an earthquake, and many places in Judea and other districts were thrown down. Thallus calls this darkness an eclipse of the sun in the third book of histories, without reason it seems to me."*[6]
- **Tertullian**, a second century Christian writer, in his *"Apologeticus"*, told the story of the crucifixion darkness and suggested that the evidence must still be held in the Roman archives.[7]
- **Phlegon of Tralles**, a second century Greek historian, also recorded the supernatural darkness, accompanied by earthquakes felt in other parts of the Empire during the reign of Tiberius (probably that of 29 CE). He wrote, *"there was the greatest eclipse of the sun and it became night in the sixth hour of the day so that stars even appeared in the heavens. There was a great earthquake in Bithynia, and many things were overturned in Nicaea."* [8] He also wrote that *"Jesus, while alive, was of no assistance to himself, but that he arose after death,*

and exhibited the marks of his punishment, and showed how his hands had been pierced by nails."[9]

The Criterion of Corroboration by Hostile Critics (Criterion 5)

The primary idea of this test is that hostile critics, (people who are outside of a particular belief system and who disagree with it), are the least likely to affirm or validate something that they are opposed to. Corroboration by hostile critics is, therefore, extremely persuasive in establishing the historical validity of a document or an event. In the case of the Biblical account of the life, miracles, death and resurrection of Jesus Christ, there are several important sources of hostile corroboration.

Firstly, there are the Roman and Greek historians already mentioned, none of whom (except for Tertullian) were Christians. As Romans and Greeks, they would have been philosophically opposed to the teachings of Christianity, yet they confirmed key events in the life of Jesus.

Secondly, and even more significantly, the Jewish sacred text, the Talmud, mentions Jesus on several occasions, even referring to his miracles. It attributes these miracles to the power of the devil and accuses Jesus of *"sorcery"*. For example, The Babylonian Talmud (BT, Sanhedrin, 43a) states,

"On the eve of the Passover Yeshua [the Nazarene] was hanged. For forty days before the execution took place a herald went forth and cried, "He is going forth to be stoned because he has practiced sorcery and enticed Israel to apostasy. Anyone who can say anything in his favour, let him come and plead on his behalf." And since nothing was brought forward in his favour, he was hanged on the eve of Passover."[10]

Significantly, even Jesus' enemies, the Jews, could not deny the power of His miracles, instead choosing to attribute them to evil sorcery.[11]

Thirdly, there is the famous reference by Flavius Josephus, a practising Jew and an outstanding first century historian. In 93 AD, in Rome, Josephus published his lauded work, "*Antiquities of the Jews*", which included the following account;

"About this time there lived Jesus, a wise man, if indeed one ought to call him a man. For he was one who performed surprising deeds and was a teacher of such people as accept the truth gladly. He won over many Jews and many of the Greeks. He was the Messiah. And when, upon the accusation of the principal men among us, Pilate had condemned him to a cross, those who had first come to love him did not cease. He appeared to them spending a third day restored to life, for the prophets of God had foretold these things and a thousand other marvels about him. And the tribe of the Christians, so called after him, has still to this day not disappeared."[12]

This passage has been embroiled in controversy since the 1700's, with atheists and sceptics arguing that the passage must be an interpolation by later Christian copyists, as a Jew would surely never have written such a favourable report of Christ. The ensuing debate throughout the subsequent centuries has generated the equivalent of a small library of academic papers and books, either defending or refuting the authenticity of this one small paragraph. In 1995, however, a discovery was published that brought important new evidence to the debate. It uncovered an earlier document that Josephus had used as a source document for his comments about Jesus, thus proving that they were not added by a later copyist.[13] While aggressive atheists still maintain that this paragraph must have been inserted by a Christian copyist, the vast majority of neutral academics are now of the opinion that the reference is largely authentic (with the possible exception of the words *"if indeed one ought to call him a man"* and *"He was the messiah"*, which are still disputed). This reference by Josephus represents a powerful corroboration by a hostile critic of the miracles of Jesus and the historicity of His resurrection.

The Criterion of Author Credibility (Criterion 6)

This test assesses the possible veracity of an ancient published work by evaluating the credibility of its author, in much the same way that academics still assess author credibility today. On this basis the New Testament books are widely regarded as works of the highest historical calibre. Luke, in particular, is held in very high regard. Sir William Mitchell Ramsay (1851-1939), the esteemed Oxford archaeologist and historian, once declared that *"Luke is a historian of the first rank; not merely are his statements of fact trustworthy...this author should be placed along with the very greatest historians."*[14] This declaration by Ramsay was not given lightly. He was raised as an atheist and was originally convinced that the Bible was fraudulent. He spent 15 years digging in the Holy Land and examining ancient documents, believing that he would disprove the New Testament accounts. Instead, he became convinced of the historical reliability of Luke's writings and became a Christian himself. He published his findings in 1895.[15] (Ramsay went on to publish a total of 18 books and dozens of academic papers confirming the historicity of the New Testament documents).[16] Josh Mc Dowell reports, *"The* publication caused a furore of dismay among the sceptics of the world. Its attitude was utterly unexpected because it was contrary to the announced intention of the author years before."[17]

William Ramsay is just one of several prominent academics and historians who have set out to disprove the story of Jesus, only to be converted themselves. In Chapter 3, I mentioned Albert Henry Ross, who wrote the landmark book, *"Who Moved The Stone?"*, under the pseudonym, Frank Morrison. I also mentioned Lee Strobel, the Chicago investigative reporter who was converted while trying to disprove the resurrection of Christ, resulting in the writing of the best seller, *"The Case For Christ"*.

But there were others. The list notably includes C. S. Lewis, a once ardent atheist who wrote of his eventual conversion, stating, *"In the Trinity Term of 1929 I gave in, and admitted that God was God, and knelt and prayed: perhaps, that night, the most dejected and reluctant convert in all England."*[18] Lewis's inability to refute the solid historical evidence for the life and resurrection of Jesus led to his reluctant conversion – a conversion that would eventually result in the publication of, arguably, the most profound Christian philosophical writings of the modern era.

THE TRANSCRIPTION RELIABILITY OF THE BIBLE

Occasionally, some within the sceptic community try to argue that the Bible's transcription (copying) process has been deeply flawed over the centuries. They claim that it must be full of transcription errors and interpolations (insertions by later copyists), resulting in a Biblical text that probably bears little resemblance to the original documents. There are three important pieces of historical evidence which refute this accusation; the meticulous copying process of the Jewish scribes, the overwhelming documentary evidence for the New Testament and, thirdly, the Dead Sea scrolls.

The Meticulous Copying Process Of The Scribes

While it is true that, for most of its long life, the Bible was copied by hand, the claim that a vast number of errors must have crept into the text ignores the extremely rigorous copying process that was instituted by the Jews. In ancient times the copying of the Old Testament was the sole task of professional scribes. The Jews revered their sacred text so highly that the copying process was conducted according to the strictest possible guidelines.

When a copy of a book of the Old Testament became worn or faded, and a new copy was ordered, a single scribe was given the task of producing the new copy. Working from the original scroll, the scribe would copy the first word of the first line, then he would put down his writing quill and pick up a pointer, called a yad. Using the yad, he would count the number of letters, jots and tittles (small grammatical marks) in the original word and then count those of the same word on the new scroll, to ensure that the new copy had exactly the same number of letters, jots and tittles. If the new word was correct, he would put down his yad, pick up his quill and copy the second word. The second word's letters, jots and tittles would then be counted and verified using the yad. This process continued for each word on the first line. When every word of the first line had been successfully copied and verified, a second verification process took place. The scribe would take up the yad and count every letter, jot and tittle in the entire first line of the of the original scroll and then undertake the same count in the first line of the original scroll. This second verification ensured that the scribe had not missed an entire word in the copying process.

This copying and verification process continued word by word and line by line, until the first page of the scroll had been completed. (Hebrew scrolls consisted of many individual pages glued together into one continuous scroll). When the last line of the first page had been successfully copied and verified, a third verification process was then undertaken. Using the yad, the scribe would then count every letter, jot and tittle on the original page and then on the copy, to verify that they were exactly the same. This ensured that the scribe had not missed copying an entire line and also provided a final verification of the entire page. If the scribe was satisfied that the copied page was identical to the original, a second scribe had to undertake the same count and corroborate the verification. Only once this final verification had taken place was the new page accepted as accurate and the scribe could proceed to copy the next page. If, at any point, a copying error was detected on a page, even if it was a single missed letter in the last word on the page, Jewish law dictated that the entire page had to be burnt, and the copying of that page had to be recommenced. This rigorous process continued throughout the entire scroll until the final page had been copied and verified.

Historians acknowledge that this rigorous copying process is the most meticulous copying process in human history[19]. In no other culture, at no other time, was the copying of documents undertaken with such obsessively meticulous attention to detail. Sceptics who claim that the Bible must be full of copying errors simply have not bothered to investigate the process by which it was copied.

The Dead Sea Scrolls

Despite the meticulous copying process of Hebrew scribes being well known among historians, sceptics continued to claim, throughout the first half of the 20th century, that gross errors must have crept into the Hebrew Scriptures over the centuries, and that we can have no way of knowing that what we read today was anything like what was originally written. The discovery of the Dead Sea Scrolls, however, silenced their accusations.

The Dead Sea Scrolls are a collection of approximately 1,000 documents, written in Hebrew, Aramaic and Greek, discovered between 1947 and 1979 in caves near Qumran on the shores of the Dead Sea, 18km east of Jerusalem and 500m below sea level.

The first manuscripts were found by a shepherd who threw a rock into a cave to chase out a goat that had strayed. When he did so, he heard the sound of breaking pottery, and went to investigate. The cave contained a collection of sealed, pottery jars. Inside the jars were ancient documents, wrapped in linen to preserve them.

There are 11 caves which were subsequently explored. Most historians believe that the caves were the monastic retreat of a Jewish Essene community (a Jewish sect) who had apparently retreated there during or shortly before the Roman purge of Israel around 70 AD. The majority of documents in the caves were parchment (animal skin) with a few papyrus documents as well. These documents represent the library of the Essene community. Cave 4, where 80% of the manuscripts were found, contained approximately 15,000 fragments (some of them very small) from 500 documents.

The documents range in date from 200 BC to about 68 AD, and include Biblical and non-Biblical books. The non-Biblical books include commentaries on the Old Testament, hymns, liturgies, accounts, monastic rules and procedures. The Biblical books comprise copies of about half the books in the Old Testament, including a copy of Isaiah which is 1000 years older than any previously discovered copy! In fact, the Dead Sea Scrolls are, to this day, the oldest collection of Old Testament books ever found.

The Dead Sea Scrolls are important because:

1. They bring us hundreds of years closer to the Old Testament autographs (the original documents, penned by the authors)

2. They show how little the Old Testament documents have changed over time - displaying only minor variations in spelling and grammar between themselves and texts hundreds of years later.

The Dead Sea Scrolls have been hailed as the greatest archaeological discovery of the 20th century.[20] For Christians they have provided unarguable, objective proof of the textual reliability of the Old Testament and the accuracy of the transmission process over millennia. The scrolls continue to be studied by scholars from around the world and continue to provide valuable help in formulating and publishing the accepted text of the Old Testament.

. . .

The Overwhelming Documentary Evidence For The New Testament

The copying of the New Testament was not always undertaken with such meticulous rigour as was the Old Testament. While some copies of New Testament books were produced by professional scribes, many others were copied by ordinary people. This was because the new Christian movement was ostracised from Judaism, and it quickly became, what we would call today, a house church movement. Thus, when for example, Paul wrote a letter to a particular church in a particular city, his letters were so prized that every household wanted a copy. The original was often passed around from household to household, and each household made their own copy. Eventually letters to specific cities and churches found their way to other cities, as Christians around the world were eager to read the letters from Paul and the other Apostles. In this way, hundreds and thousands of copies were produced all around the ancient world. Those who produced the new copies were not usually trained scribes, but were ordinary people, like you and I, with varying literary abilities. This often resulted in incidental copying errors. Words were misspelt. Words were occasionally omitted. Sometimes a whole line was accidently skipped. If a flawed copy was then passed on and copied, these errors were perpetuated in subsequent copies, and so errors tended to accumulate.

While this might seem extremely problematic, the vast number of surviving copies of these ancient New Testament documents allows textual critics to examine varying versions (known as variants) of a New Testament passage and ascertain, to within a very high degree of certainty, the exact wording of the original text. Textual critics are like textual detectives who piece together the wording of the autographic (original) text. In most cases this is relatively easy to do. Using dating techniques, textual critics can document families back through time, identifying when variants were introduced to the text and arriving at the precise wording via corroboration with other similarly aged texts.

An example might help to illustrate. In Ephesians 5:31 there are four variants among the surviving manuscripts:

1. *"For this reason a man leaves father and mother and clings to **his** wife"*
2. *"For this reason a man leaves father and mother and clings to **the** wife"*
3. *"For this reason a man leaves father and mother and **joins** the wife"*
4. *"For this reason a man leaves father and mother"*.

Using dating techniques and comparing the textual family lines of each of these variants, textual critics can determine which of these variants was the original text and can even determine, to within a decade or two, when each of the variants was introduced to the textual record. Accordingly, it is the first version that is recognised as autographic (from the pen of the author) and is published in our modern Bibles.

Compared to other books of antiquity, no other literary work comes close to approaching the New Testament in terms of manuscript evidence and close time span between the autograph (the original document) and the earliest extant copies (copies still in existence). The table below reveals how extraordinarily well-attested the New Testament is when compared to other ancient works. Note the extremely small time-gap between the date of the original writing and the date of the earliest surviving copies of the New Testament. Note, also, the extraordinary number of surviving Greek manuscripts of the

New Testament, which allows scholars to ascertain the exact wording of the original texts with great accuracy.

Author	Date Written	Earliest Surviving Copy	Time Span between original & surviving copy	No. of Copies
Pliny	61-113 A.D.	850 A.D.	750 yrs	7
Plato	427-347 B.C.	900 A.D.	1200 yrs	7
Demosthenes	4th Cent. B.C.	1100 A.D.	800 yrs	8
Herodotus	480-425 B.C.	900 A.D.	1300 yrs	8
Suetonius	75-160 A.D.	950 A.D.	800 yrs	8
Thucydides	460-400 B.C.	900 A.D.	1300 yrs	8
Euripides	480-406 B.C.	1100 A.D.	1300 yrs	9
Aristophanes	450-385 B.C.	900 A.D.	1200 yrs	10
Caesar	100-44 B.C.	900 A.D.	1000 yrs	10
Tacitus	100 A.D.	1100 A.D.	1000 yrs	20
Aristotle	384-322 B.C.	1100 A.D.	1400 yrs	49
Sophocles	496-406 B.C.	1000 A.D.	1400 yrs	193
Homer (Iliad)	900 B.C.	400 B.C.	500 yrs	643
New Testament	50-100 A.D.	c. 115 - 135 A.D.	15-40 yrs	5600 Greek MS

The extraordinary manuscript attestation of the New Testament, together with the temporal proximity of surviving manuscripts to the autographs is unparalleled in ancient literature. This allows textual critics to arrive at an accepted precise wording of each verse of the Bible with an extremely high degree of certainty.

The Bible, as a reliable historical document, stands head and shoulders above all other literary works from antiquity. We can have great confidence that the words we read today are the words that were originally penned by the authors.

Furthermore, the credibility of the Biblical narrative is corroborated by the universally accepted Criteria of Historical Credibility (previously outlined). This includes significant corroboration by external, independent historical sources, as well as the startling lack of protestation by hostile critics.

Most importantly, the life, miracles, death, and resurrection of Jesus Christ are supported by overwhelming and convincing historical evidence. Those who deny Christ's existence or claim mythological embellishment are either unaware of the hard evidence to the contrary, or are choosing to ignore it.

For those who are earnestly seeking God, you will find Him in the person of Jesus Christ, as He is revealed to you in Holy Scripture.

Reflection Questions

1. *What new insights have you gained from this chapter? Has this chapter changed any of your views?*

2. *What questions or challenges has this chapter raised for you?*

3. *Read 2 Timothy 3:16. What does this tell us about the Bible? What are the four specific applications identified in this verse?*

4. *Read Isaiah 40:8 and 1 Peter 1:25. What are these verses proclaiming? What application might this have for our understanding of God's supervision of the transmission of the Bible?*

5. *Read Hebrews chapter 1. This is an incredibly rich passage. What does it reveal about Jesus – His person and work?*

6. *Read 1 Peter 3:15. How should this verse guide us as we seek to engage in dialogue with seekers and sceptics?*

SIX

THE PROBLEM OF SUFFERING

The existence of terrible suffering and evil in our world is arguably the strongest rebuttal against the existence of God in the atheist's arsenal. Without doubt, the scope and magnitude of human suffering poses significant problems in seeking to reconcile our painful reality with the existence of an all-powerful, loving God. For it is undeniable that the universe contains vast amounts of misery. Every 5 seconds, somewhere in the world, a child dies of starvation. Every minute, 25 people die because of a lack of clean drinking water. Every hour, 700 people die of malaria. In recent years we have witnessed earthquakes in the Himalayas that killed 50,000 people and left 3 million homeless, and a tsunami in Thailand that killed

300,000 people in one devastating inundation. Where is God in all this?

John Stott, noted theologian, states,

"The fact of suffering undoubtedly constitutes the single greatest challenge to the Christian faith. Its distribution and degree appear to be entirely random and therefore unfair. Sensitive spirits ask if it can possibly be reconciled with God's justice and love."[1]

The ancient Greek philosopher, Epicurus, was one of the first to propose suffering as a logical argument for the non-existence of God. He stated,

"Either God wants to abolish evil, and cannot; or He can, but does not want to; or He cannot and does not want to. If He wants to, but cannot, He is impotent. If He can, and does not want to, He is wicked. But if God both can and wants to abolish evil, then how comes evil in the world?"[2]

The 18th century Scottish sceptic David Hume, expressed it more succinctly,

"Is He willing to prevent evil, but not able? Then He is impotent. Is He able, but not willing? Then He is malevolent. Is He both able and willing? Whence then is evil?"[3]

NO LOGICAL CONTRADICTION

Many sceptics propose the above deductive line of reasoning to claim a logical contradiction between the existence of both suffering and an omnipotent, good God. However, no such contradiction exists explicitly. In order for there to be an inherent logical inconsistency, at least one further assumption has to be made.

Either:
An omnipotent God could create a world in which there was no suffering
OR
A good God could not have morally justifiable reasons for permitting suffering

Sceptics are appealing to one or both of these assumptions when they use the issue of suffering as a means of arguing against the existence of God. If either of these assumptions can be shown to be true, then they could be justified in consigning the Christian concept of God to the realm of myth. But sceptics are a long way from proving either of these two assumptions. In fact, as we shall see, both assumptions are inherently, logically flawed. Approaching this topic from a purely logical perspective leads us to the inescapable conclusion that, far from being a contradiction of God's existence, suffering is actually a necessity if we are to have a universe that is meaningful.

THE LOGICAL NECESSITY OF SUFFERING

We cannot have free will without the possibility of evil and, hence, suffering. Quite simply, it is a logical impossibility for free will to exist without the possibility of choosing to use that free will for evil. If there is no possibility of disobedience to God, if the only option is obedience, then free will simply does not exist. Those who claim that if an omnipotent God exists, He could have created a world without suffering, are correct in one sense. God could have created a world without the possibility of suffering, but this would necessitate a robotically preprogrammed humanity, unable to make free choices, which, in turn, would render any notion of love meaningless. This is because the concept of love only has meaning if it is freely given as a choice of the will, rather than a product of preprogramed spiritual coding.

Additionally, the proposition that an omnipotent (infinitely powerful) God can do anything, is false. While it is true that *"with God all things are possible"* (Matt 19:26), intrinsic, logical impossibilities are not *things*, but theoretical non-entities. God can do anything except those things that are logically contradictory. For example, God cannot make a round square. Nor can He create a rock that is too heavy for Him to lift. In the same way, He cannot create humans with free will while at the same time making it impossible for them to disobey Him. The great C. S. Lewis, in his profound book, *"The Problem of Pain"*, writes,

"God's Omnipotence means power to do all that is intrinsically possible, not to do the intrinsically impossible. You may attribute miracles to Him, but not nonsense. This is no limit to His power. ... It is no more possible for God than for the weakest of His creatures to carry out both of two mutually exclusive alternatives; not because His power meets an obstacle, but because nonsense remains nonsense even when we talk it about God."[4]

Lewis extrapolates this concept further;

"Try to exclude the possibility of suffering which the order of nature and the existence of free wills involve, and you will find that you have excluded life itself."[5]

It is possible, perhaps, to conceive of a world in which God continually intercedes to nullify the harmful consequences of mankind's free will; a world where He turns an assassin's bullet to jelly after it is fired; where a baseball bat turns to straw before it connects with someone's skull; where a violent husband's fist is halted one centimetre before connecting with his wife's face; where a hurtful comment is transformed into an expression of love before it enters the ears of the hearer; where a grossly inadequate wage is boosted magically into an adequate payment in the worker's bank account; where the imbalance of the earth's resources due to greed and selfishness is magically readjusted every night. But such a world would be a complete nonsense, for it would mean that the laws of nature, and even matter itself, would constantly behave unpredictably. It would also effectively nullify free will, for in such a world every evil action would be constantly thwarted. Language would have no meaning, because what I said would not necessarily be what was heard, and even evil thoughts would be wiped away before they formed.

In a recent conversation with a sceptic, I was explaining the inevitability of suffering as a result of its inherent link to free will. He responded by saying,"*If those who go to heaven will not be robotic in their love for God and in their obedience to Him, if they will still have free will, but sin will no longer be possible for them in heaven, why didn't God create this kind of world in the first place?*" It is a very good question, but I think there is a rational answer.

The Bible does not speak of people having truly unfettered free will in heaven, and there is a logical reason for that. To be fully in the presence of the transcendent, omnipotent Creator God, will be to have our senses completely overwhelmed with His glory, power and majesty. It will be such a soul-shaking, awe-inspiring experience that the concept of rebelling against

Him or disobeying Him will be completely unthinkable. Sin will not be possible in heaven, not because our free wills will be removed, but because they will be completely overpowered by the gloriously awe-full presence of God. For this very reason, God does not currently disclose His full glory to mankind, for it would compromise our free wills. No one would be able to resist Him; everyone would be driven to submit to Him by the overwhelming, irresistible force of His power and glory. God values our choice too much to force Himself on us in this way. He wants us to want Him, not as a result of being overwhelmed by Him, but out of the sincere desire of our hearts. He wants our love to be genuine, freely chosen, and not manipulated or coerced by the power of His presence.

THE ONTOLOGICAL ANTECEDENT OF SUFFERING

While the existence of free will necessitates the possibility of suffering, it can only explain suffering that has an explicit human cause. Suffering that is directly caused by the wrongful use of human free will, however, only accounts for one component of suffering. The natural world is filled with suffering that is not directly caused by mankind's evil actions; hurricanes, earthquakes, floods, droughts, diseases and terrible accidents. It is at this point that we must turn to the Biblical account of the Fall, to understand the ontological antecedent of suffering within the natural world.

In Genesis 2 and 3, we read the account of the Fall of mankind. I briefly referred to this in Chapter 3, but now let us explore it more fully. Whether or not you regard this story as a literal historical event (as I do) does not affect its relevance for our exploration of the antecedent of natural suffering. At its simplest level, the Biblical account of the Fall indicates that, at some point in the distant past, mankind rebelled against God. Whether or not you believe that a piece of fruit was involved, makes no difference for our present discussion. The fact remains that mankind is currently in a state of open rebellion against God, and the Bible says that this had a specific beginning at a point in history. The serious nature of this rebellion cannot be understated. It involved a deliberate refusal to be governed by the commands of God, and a desire to be masters of our own destiny. It was a heinous act of self-will, refusing to accept our creaturely status, thereby cutting the intrinsic ties that bound our spirits, in subservient intimacy, to God's Spirit. The cutting of that tie, the breaking of that spiritual cord, had devastating impacts upon the physical world. Consider the avalanche of profound consequences that immediately followed, declared to Adam and Eve by God in Genesis 3:

- Pain in childbirth (v.16)
- Thorns and weeds will now plague mankind (v.18)
- Work would now be hard and painful (v.19)
- Mere survival would be difficult (v.17)
- Death became the destiny of us all (v.19)
- We were cast out from the immediate presence of God (v.23)

Bible scholars point out that these pronouncements by God were by no means exhaustive; they were the briefest of summaries of the vast and profound change that came over the entire physical universe the moment the first humans sinned. Our sin was so horrendously evil that it affected the entire physical universe, down to the sub-atomic level. The universe itself became sick, broken and dysfunctional - infected with our sin. Paul describes this profound brokenness in Romans 8 when he says that creation is now *"in bondage to decay"* (v.21) and that *"the whole of creation is groaning"* (v.22). The physical universe is profoundly sick, and we made it so!

How could this be? How could the surreptitious eating of a simple piece of fruit ruin the entire universe? The answer is that the physical universe was connected to God through the subservient rulership of mankind. In Genesis 1:26 we read, *"Then God said, 'Let us make man in our image, after our likeness. And let them have dominion over the fish of the sea and over the birds of the heavens and over the livestock and over all the earth and over every creeping thing that creeps on the earth'."* (Genesis 1:26). God gave mankind *"dominion ... over all the earth"*. We were appointed the rulers of the physical creation, to have *dominion* over it. As long as we remained in a right relationship with God, His providential power would flow unimpeded into every molecule of the universe, ensuring its perfect functioning. But when we severed the cord of our subservience, we not only "fell" from grace ourselves, and began to die, but we took the whole of creation with us. It was wilful rebellion against the God who created the universe and who reigns at its centre, upholding its laws and constants. That first, seemingly simple act of disobedience, represented a seismic shift in the spiritual balance of the universe. The creature said to the Creator, *"No! I will not obey you! I will not recognise your right to tell me how to live!"* The cataclysmic shock of this treasonous act reverberated through every molecule of the universe, destroying its perfect balance.

A.W. Tozer explains the serious nature of sin and its universal consequences;

"Sin is a capital crime as well. It is treason against the great God Almighty who made the heavens and the earth. Sin is a crime against the moral order of the universe. Each time a man or woman strikes against God's moral nature and kingdom, he or she acts against the moral government of the entire universe."[6]

The spiritual and physical realms are inextricably entwined in a way that we can only dimly perceive – bound together in a celestial dance that is perfectly balanced, as long as God is enthroned at its centre. When mankind rebelled against the Creator, the physical realm became tainted with our rebellion; infected with a profound spiritual sickness that has corrupted the universe at its core. Every natural disaster that has since ensued, every disease and illness, every accident, every hard, painful day of toil, every death, every heartache – all this and more - is our fault. Our sin has destroyed the perfect balance of creation.

God's "curse" in Genesis 3 was not a list of arbitrary punishments, but a pronouncement to Adam and Eve of the profound consequences in the physical world that would inevitably flow from their betrayal. It was God's declaration of the profound brokenness of His beautiful creation, caused by the evil of our rebellion against Him. In this sense, there is no such thing as a "natural" disaster. There is nothing natural about them; they are decidedly unnatural. The physical world was never created to behave as it does now. Every instance of sickness and physical calamity is a symptom of a world that is broken, that is diseased at its very core.

Therefore, all suffering in the natural world, including death itself, is ultimately due to our sin. Romans 5:12 states that *"sin entered the world through one man, and death through sin"*. Much has been written surrounding this one verse, with varying interpretations concerning the scope and application of the word *"death"*. I interpret this verse quite literally. Prior to mankind's sin, the physical world was perfect, and nothing died, not even an insect. The horrifically violent nature of the natural world today, owes its existence to the treasonous act of the original humans who, by severing the bond that bound them to their Creator, plunged the world into darkness and chaos.

THE REMEDIAL NECESSITY OF SUFFERING

Having established that all suffering is either directly or indirectly the result of mankind's sin, one must pose the question as to why God does not intervene more often to alleviate our suffering. Surely a compassionate God would want to rescue His creatures from the extremes of suffering? The Bible provides an ultimate answer to this question: God has promised to eventually remove all suffering from the world, when He recreates the universe in its original splendour and perfection. The prophecy of Revelation states, *"Then I saw a new heaven and a new earth, for the first heaven and the first earth had passed away"* (Rev 21:1). The reference to a new *"heaven"*, is a reference to the Jewish concept of the first and second levels of "heaven" – the realm of the stars and planets. In other words, the Bible prophesies that the entire universe will be recreated in perfection at the end of history. That is good news! The bad news, however, is that in order for God to remove all suffering from His wounded universe, He will need to remove the cause of that suffering, by bringing all mankind to judgment and finally ending our rebellion eternally! To those who demand that God ends all suffering, I often respond by saying, *"You have no idea what you're asking for! I don't think you really want Him to do that just yet - because that would mean bringing you to judgment!"*

We must also acknowledge that our concept of God's divine goodness is flawed. The fact that God allows the current state of affairs to continue seems, to some people, irreconcilable with a God who is intrinsically good. How can a good God allow people to suffer? It is at this point that we must acknowledge our limitations. C. S. Lewis comments,

"Any consideration of the goodness of God, at once threatens us with the following dilemma... If God is wiser than we, His judgment must differ from ours on many things, and not least on good and evil. What seems to us good may therefore not be good in His eyes, and what seems to us evil may not be evil."[7]

The Bible indicates that there are times when God may permit suffering in order to achieve a greater good within the individual. The Scriptures speak of the refining work that suffering accomplishes within the sufferer, producing perseverance (Jas 1:2-4), and restored fellowship with God (Heb 12:1-6). The Apostle Peter explains how God may sometimes use suffering to refine us;

"In all this you greatly rejoice, though now for a little while you may have had to suffer grief in all kinds of trials. These have come so that the proven genuineness of your faith—of greater worth than gold, which perishes even though refined by fire—may result in praise, glory and honour when Jesus Christ is revealed" (1 Peter 1:6-7).

Thus, on at least some occasions, suffering plays a remedial role in the life of the Christian – causing us to rely more intimately upon God's strength and drawing us into closer fellowship with Him. C. S. Lewis famously stated, *"God whispers to us in our pleasures, speaks in our conscience, but shouts in our pains."*[8] Certainly, many Christians can testify to the way God used suffering to help them see what is truly important in life and to draw them closer to God.

This accords with our own experience of human goodness. Pain and suffering are often required in order to bring about a greater good. The temporary discomfort and suffering of going to the dentist is necessary in order remediate potentially serious infections before they spread further. A mother who takes her baby to the doctor for a vaccine injection is deliberately causing her baby pain, knowing that it is necessary in order to bring about a greater good. The fact that the baby has no idea why pain is being inflicted upon her does not mean that a good reason does not exist. So it is with us and God.

THE PROVIDENTIAL NECESSITY OF SUFFERING

Whereas the remedial necessity of suffering refers to the way in which God sometimes uses suffering to bring about a greater good within the sufferer, the providential necessity of suffering refers to God's use of suffering to bring about His wider purposes globally.

From our limited human perspective, we simply cannot conceptualise the ripple effect that our individual suffering may have upon others and upon events in subsequent history. We see this ripple effect illustrated in the newly developing field of Chaos Theory,[9] where scientists have discovered that certain macroscopic systems, such as weather systems or insect populations, can be dramatically impacted by the smallest, seemingly unrelated events, often on the other side of the globe. A small stream being dammed in Africa can set in motion a chain of events that leads to a hurricane in the Atlantic or the extinction of a species in Europe.

In the spiritual world, we have no idea how our seemingly pointless sufferings may have far reaching impact for the Kingdom of God. My own experience can testify to this. The death of my mother when I was 10 years old set in motion a chain of events that led to me becoming a Christian at the age of 16, which in turn has had ongoing ripple effects through the ministries that I have had. Similarly, a friend of mine, Howard, died of cancer when we were both 18 years old. He was a strong Christian and during his final months he wrote many poems and drew some beautiful artwork expressing his profound faith in the goodness of God. After his death Howard's poems and drawings were published in a book called, "*Lord, You Are My Friend*". Although, at the time of Howard's death, many people questioned the goodness of God in allowing such a vibrant young man to die so young, in the years since, many people have come to faith through Howard's lasting testimony.

We simply do not know how God is going to use our suffering to impact others. Both my mother and Howard died without knowing how God would use their suffering. We may never perceive the reasons for our suffering while we are alive either, but this does not necessarily infer that our suffering has no meaning. Romans 8:28 assures us that *"in all things God works for the good of those who love Him and are called according to His purpose"*.

THE ESCHATOLOGICAL NECESSITY OF SUFFERING

Eschatology refers to the theology of the end times. God has a grand plan that He is working towards. More than merely impacting individual lives in the present, God is weaving his purposes throughout human history to ultimately bring the entire universe back under the sovereign rule of Christ. Ephesians 1:10, refers to *"God's purpose in Christ, to be put into effect when the times reach their fulfillment – to bring everything together in heaven and on earth under Christ"*. Nothing that happens in our world can spoil God's plan, for He can weave every event into the fabric of His unfolding purposes. This includes our suffering. The ripple effect of our suffering can not only extend to people in another part of the world, but may also extend to other epochs of history.

Theologian and philosopher, William Lane Craig comments;

"Certainly, many evils seem pointless and unnecessary to us – but we are simply not in a position to judge. The brutal murder of an innocent man or a child's dying of leukemia could send a ripple effect through history so that God's morally sufficient reason for permitting it might not emerge until centuries later or perhaps in another country... Once we contemplate God's providence over the whole of history, then it becomes evident how hopeless it is for limited observers to speculate on the probability of God having morally sufficient reasons for the evils that we see. We simply are not in a good position to assess such probabilities with confidence."[10]

The sufferings and imprisonment of both the Apostle Paul and the Apostle John are powerful examples of God's eschatological purposes in allowing suffering. Both Paul and John were incarcerated unjustly and locked away from the outside world for years at a time. Anyone who has been to prison for even a few brief months will testify to the life-shattering experience that this can be. Why did God allow His faithful servants to be so badly treated? Many 1st century Christians almost certainly pondered that very question. From our perspective 2,000 years later, however, we have the privilege of reading several beautiful and profound books of Scripture that were written by these men during their imprisonment (Ephesians, Philippians, Colossians, Philemon and Revelation). Because Paul and John were unable visit the churches under their care, they were forced to write letters; letters which found their way into Holy Scripture and which will continue to guide and inspire people until the consummation of God's Kingdom. Did the Apostles realise how God was using their imprisonment? Did they have any concept that the words they scribbled in their cold, lonely dungeons would be inspiring people for thousands of years to come? Probably not. But such is the eschatological providence of the God who holds the whole of human history in His hands.

THE TRANSCENDENT NECESSITY OF SUFFERING

If we assume that the God who created the universe is a transcendent being whose wisdom and power are infinitely greater than ours, (which is a reasonable assumption, given the mind-boggling scale and grandeur of the universe), then it would be naive in the extreme to presume that His purposes and thought processes would be completely discernible and understandable to limited creatures such as ourselves. In fact, the scenario with the highest probability is that any God who is capable of creating all the matter in the universe from nothing - who is able to design billions of galaxies with quadrillions of stars across an expanse of untold billions of lightyears - will be so incomprehensively superior to us that our feeble brains will be incapable of apprehending all but the vaguest notions of His nature and His purposes. In other words, if this transcendent God is infinitely powerful and infinitely wise, it follows that many of His purposes and actions will be infinitely beyond our ability to comprehend. We have less chance of completely understanding God than an ant has of understanding astrophysics! The possibility of inscrutable higher purposes undergirding the existence of suffering are, therefore, deducibly certain. Those who claim that God cannot possibly have valid reasons for permitting suffering, fail to appreciate our laughably inadequate ability as frail humans to understand the higher purposes of an infinite, transcendent God.

THE CONTEXT OF GOD'S UNSEEN INTERVENTIONS

As well as the various ways that suffering may be necessary in a meaningful and purposive universe, we must also consider the problem of suffering in the context of several other factors. One of those is the very real possibility that our world would be infinitely worse than it is, except for the constant restraining hand of God, continually intervening to keep us from sliding into unthinkable chaos. Who knows how many times God intervenes to avert disaster and protect people from danger, without us realising? The very fact that you are still alive today and reading this book may be because, yesterday, God averted a disaster that would otherwise have befallen you. You aren't aware of it because it didn't happen! Only in eternity will we become aware of how much and how often God has intervened in our lives and in human history to stop things getting even worse. Without God's restraining hand, our world may well have spiralled into a violent darkness far more chaotic than we can imagine. Those who criticise God for allowing the suffering that He does, are only looking at one side of the equation.

THE CONTEXT OF DEMONIC ACTIVITY

One cannot discuss the problem of suffering without referring to the book of Job. It is an extraordinary account of God allowing Satan to inflict the most horrendous suffering upon a righteous man, killing his family, destroying all his possessions and devastating his health. The purpose of the suffering was hidden from Job, but it seems to have revolved around God proving that Satan could not destroy the faith of those whom God has sealed. It is difficult to determine to what extent the satanic causes of suffering, indicated in the book of Job, are either normative or exceptional. At the very least, however, it is apparent that Satan is, on at least some occasions, able to cause sickness, suffering and even death. We should not underestimate the violent and evil nature of Satan's rebellion against God that is being played out in the physical universe. Part of his rebellion manifests itself in a determined effort to ruin everything that is good, including destroying the quality of human life. He delights in sickness, violence, addiction, squalor, injustice, abuse, misery and death.

That sickness and suffering are sometimes caused by the devil is beyond dispute. In Luke 13, Jesus declared that the woman he had healed of a crippling disease had been *"crippled by a spirit"* (Luke 13:11) and he referred to her as the woman *"whom Satan had kept bound for 18 long years"* (Luke 13:16). In Peter's sermon at Cornelius' house he states that Jesus *"went around healing all who were under the power of the devil"* (Acts 10:38).

Scripture does not indicate the normalcy or otherwise of demonically caused suffering, nor does it explain why God allows demons such latitude. One can only speculate that God is allowing demonic rebellion to run its course in the same way that he is allowing human rebellion to run its course. At the same time, He remains sovereign, at times possibly intervening in ways we do not see, and ensuring that nothing happens to thwart His ultimate purposes of redeeming a people for Himself and restoring His creation to perfection.

THE CONTEXT OF ETERNITY

Although we must not minimise the seriousness of suffering that many people endure, the Bible asks us to view the hardships of our temporal existence in the light of the inconceivably great rewards that await God's people in eternity. Paul writes, *"No eye has seen, no ear has heard, no mind has conceived what God has prepared for those who love Him"* (1 Cor 2:9). In the light of these eternal rewards, Paul exhorts God's people;

"Therefore, we do not lose heart. Though outwardly we are

wasting away, yet inwardly we are being renewed day by day. For our light and momentary troubles are achieving for us an eternal glory that far outweighs them all. So we fix our eyes not on what is seen, but on what is unseen, since what is seen is temporary, but what is unseen is eternal." (2 Cor 4:16-18)

Significantly, Paul, the one writing these words, has, by this time, suffered horrendous cruelty and hardships. On five separate occasions he was scourged with a triple-thonged whip, just for preaching the gospel. The ends of the typical whip used by 1st century Romans had bits of bone tied to the end in order to tear the flesh of the victim and inflict maximum pain. On each of the five occasions when Paul was whipped, he would have been given the standard 26 lashes to his back and 13 to his breast, resulting in profound injury and permanent scarring. On three other occasions, Paul was stripped and beaten by Roman soldiers with wooden rods. On one occasion, when he was preaching in Lystra, he was attacked by an angry mob who then stoned him and dragged his unconscious body outside the city gates, leaving him for dead. Paul's body would have been a mass of scars! He referred to these scars when he wrote to the churches in Galatia, *"Finally, let no one cause me trouble, for I bear on my body the marks of Jesus."* (Gal 6:17). As well as beatings, Paul was cruelly imprisoned several times, bound hand and foot in chains. He also suffered from natural disasters. He was shipwrecked on three occasions, and on one of those occasions he was adrift in the ocean for a day and a night before being rescued. Paul also wrote of being in constant danger from bandits, from Romans and from his own countrymen who were trying to kill him. On top of all this Paul says that he often went without food, and was sometimes forced to live in the open without protection from the elements. (Paul lists all these horrific incidents in 2 Corinthians 11:16-33).

Can you imagine how traumatic just one or two of those events would be? Paul's life was a litany of terrible suffering! You could be excused for thinking that this man was cursed by God! Yet despite everything that Paul had endured, when he considered the future glory that awaits those who are in Christ Jesus, Paul described his sufferings as *"light and momentary troubles"* (2 Cor 4:17). This is the perspective that we all need to develop. If we are focused purely on this life, our suffering can seem overwhelming. But compared to the eternal joy of heaven, our temporal sufferings, even those that serve no obvious purpose, represent an infinitesimally small blip in the scope of our existence. Christians are called to live with this eternal perspective in mind; to have our eyes fixed on the things that are yet to come:

"And I heard a loud voice from the throne saying, "Look! God's dwelling place is now among the people, and He will dwell with them. They will be His people, and God Himself will be with them and be their God. 4 'He will wipe every tear from their eyes. There will be no more death or mourning or crying or pain, for the old order of things has passed away." (Rev 21:3-4)

THE CONTEXT OF CHANCE

A further factor needs to be incorporated into our theology of suffering (our theodicy) if we are to make sense of our world; the fact that randomness and chance play a significant role in the occurrence of suffering. This is not a particularly comfortable thought for those Christians who interpret the Bible's teaching regarding the sovereignty of God to mean that He is ordaining and purposing every instance of suffering in our world. Those who hold such a view are left clinging to the belief that nothing happens by chance; that every misery, heartache and illness in our world occurs at the specific behest of God, who somehow needs these things to take place, and specifically ordains that they should take place, in order to fulfil His purposes.

Theologian David Bentley Hart comments;

"There is, of course, some comfort to be derived from the thought that everything that occurs is governed not only by a transcendent providence, but by a universal teleology that makes every instance of pain and loss an indispensable moment in a grand scheme whose ultimate synthesis will justify all things. But consider the price at which that comfort is purchased: it requires us to believe in and love a God whose good ends will be realised not only in spite of - but entirely by way of - every cruelty, every fortuitous misery, every catastrophe, every betrayal, every sin the world has ever known; it requires us to believe in the eternal spiritual necessity of a child dying an agonizing death from diphtheria, of a young mother ravaged by cancer, of tens of thousands of Asians swallowed in an instant by the sea, of millions murdered in death camps and gulags. It seems a strange thing to find peace in a universe rendered morally intelligible at the cost of a God rendered morally loathsome."[11]

The Calvinist view, that God is specifically pulling the strings in order to orchestrate every instance of misery in our world, not only renders Him morally loathsome, but also defies common sense. Last winter, my wife caught a cold, but I did not. This was not because God had ordained it to be so, but simply because, at a certain point, my wife breathed a cold virus up her nose and I did not! It was a product of randomness and chance. God is not sitting on high, deciding whom He will give a cold to every winter! Yesterday my granddaughter fell over and grazed her knee because she tripped on a pebble. God did not place that pebble in her way or cause her to trip. He did not need her to trip in order to carry out his grand plan for humanity. Last night I stubbed my toe as I walked to the bathroom. Yesterday I developed a sore knee while going on my 5km morning jog. The day before yesterday I dropped a piece of bread with peanut butter on it, and it landed peanut butter side down on the floor. Several days ago, I bent the mower deck on my ride-on mower because I misjudged a corner, and I subsequently had to spend several hours removing the deck and bending it back into shape. To suggest that God was behind all these "calamities", or that He required them all to happen as part of His perfect will for me and for mankind is simply absurd. Randomness and chance play a large part in our daily lives.

While it is relatively easy to accept that randomness and chance play a part in these kinds of relatively insignificant inconveniences, I also believe that chance is often the determining factor in much more serious instances of suffering. For example, cancer occurs when the DNA of a cell is damaged, either through genetic replication errors during cell division or by external factors such as damage to a segment of the DNA by toxins or ultraviolet radiation. DNA damage and replication errors occur constantly in cell reproduction within our bodies, but in the vast majority of cases these mutations are either repaired by the cell or are relatively harmless. Occasionally, however, the damage to the cell's DNA occurs at a point in the genome that controls cell reproduction, and it triggers the cell to "go rogue" - to multiply uncontrollably. This is cancer. Randomness plays a huge part in this process. The 3.2 billion base pairs that comprise our double-helix DNA are almost never perfectly copied into the new cell during cell division and reproduction. Some scientists estimate that a newly divided single cell can contain up to 120,000 replication errors that need to be corrected by the cell by means of an initial repair phase known as "proofreading", and a secondary correction phase referred to as "mismatch repair". During this two-phase repair process, polymerase enzymes act upon a new cell's DNA, realigning mismatched nucleotides and adjusting incorrectly copied DNA segments until the whole double helix is an exact replica of the original. But this process is not perfect. Some mistakes "slip through the net" and are perpetuated in subsequent generations of the cell. The precise location of these unfixed errors within the 3.2 billion base pairs of the DNA strand will determine whether the cell will survive at all, and, if it does, whether it will function normally. In extremely rare cases, the damage or replication errors occur at a segment of the DNA which triggers uncontained cell division, thereby turning the cell cancerous. And all this is the product of pure chance.

How do we reconcile this to our understanding of the sovereignty of God? Many Christians would argue that if God is completely sovereign, as the Bible indicates, then surely everything that happens must be His will and, therefore, must be specifically ordained or purposed by Him. They believe that God's sovereignty excludes the possibility of the operation of random chance in our universe. It is at this point that many Christians misunderstand the nature of God's sovereignty and confuse His *perfect* will with His *permissive* will.

God's sovereignty over creation is undisputed:

"I am God and there is none like me. I know the end from the beginning, from ancient times, and what is yet to come. My purpose will stand, and I will do all that I please." (Isa 46:9-10).

God's sovereignty means that His purposes will not be thwarted. He watches over everything to ensure that nothing will derail His purposes for mankind and for the unfolding of His kingdom. Hence, Job states, *"No purpose of yours can be thwarted"* (Job 42:2). Yet we must not infer from this that everything that happens within our world is exactly as God would want it at every moment. God is not pulling **every** string **all** the time. God's will is not always done; people sin and break His commandments regularly.

God's perfect will is described in Ezekiel 18:23; *"The Lord does not desire the death of a sinner, but that all should turn to Him and live"*. This is God's perfect will. But most of the time it does not happen. And God *allows* it to not happen; He *permits* people to exercise their free wills to disobey Him. Thus, theologians speak of God's *permissive* will as distinct from His *perfect* will. David Bentley Hart states;

"What God permits, rather than violate the autonomy of the created world, may often be in itself contrary to what He wills."[12]

If we consider just human behaviour alone, we must concede that a very large percentage of human behaviour is directly contrary to God's perfect will, yet the Bible still speaks of God as being completely sovereign. Similarly, a very large percentage of the chance events in our broken physical world also fall outside of the perfect parameters that God designed in the beginning, yet God, in His sovereignty, allows them to unfold.

God's sovereignty, therefore, is one of watchful oversight with a minimalist approach to intervention. He allows both the evil actions of disobedient people and the harmful random actions of a fallen world to unfold under His watchful eye, only intervening when these things might derail his eternal purposes. This kind of minimalist, watchful sovereignty is indicated in many of the Psalms, such as Psalm 33:14 which declares that *"the Lord watches over all who live on the earth"*.

The application of this discussion of God's sovereignty to our topic of suffering is that randomness and chance often play a significant part in our suffering, yet this does not contradict the sovereignty God in any way. God sees all and knows all before it even happens. The fact that often God allows the negative outworking of random chance, rather than intervening to stop it, means that He has decided that the resulting consequences do not derail His eternal purposes.

Furthermore, we have the added promise, already stated in this chapter, that God can use the suffering and evil in our world to actually bring about His good purposes (Rom 8:28). But let us be very sure that we don't take this verse for a longer drive than it is licensed for! We must not infer from this verse that God *brings about* suffering and evil, or that He *needs* the suffering and evil to take place in order to achieve His ends. David Bentley Hart states;

"Evil can have no proper role to play in God's determination of himself or purpose for his creatures, even if by economy God can bring good from evil; it can in no way supply any imagined deficiency in God's plans; it has no essential contribution to make."[13]

So, what is the upshot of all this? Whether I catch a cold, or stub my toe, or have a tree branch fall on my head, or develop cancer, I must not claim that this is part of God's perfect will for my life. These things almost certainly arise as a result of the randomness and chance occurrences of a fallen, broken world. They are not an essential part of God's plan for my life that He has purposed for me from eternity. The fact that God knew about these calamities from eternity and, in His sovereignty, has chosen not to intervene to stop them, tells me, firstly, that they do not pose a threat to His good purposes, and, secondly, that God has decided to bring good out of them - perhaps in ways that I may not fully perceive in this life.

THE CONTEXT OF THE CROSS

Those who accuse God of aloof indifference towards human suffering, ignore God's insertion into our suffering via the cross. To those who demand of God, *"Where were you when I was suffering?"*, God replies, *"I was dying for you on the cross."* There can be no greater sign of God's great love for mankind than that the Creator of the universe should step down from His eternal transcendence and submit himself to a torturous physical death and spiritual torment in order to save people from their sins. That God should punish Himself in order to forgive us is truly shocking. In fact, other religions cannot conceive of a God who would do that.

John Stott reflects on the significance of the cross for our understanding of suffering:

"I could never myself believe in God, if it were not for the cross. In the real world of pain, how could one worship a God who was immune to it? I have entered many Buddhist temples in different Asian countries and stood respectfully before the statue of the Buddha, his legs crossed, arms folded, eyes closed,

the ghost of a smile playing round his mouth, a remote look on his face, detached from the agonies of the world. But each time after a while I have had to turn away. And in imagination I have turned instead to that lonely, twisted, tortured figure on the cross, nails through hands and feet, back lacerated, limbs wrenched, brow bleeding from thorn-pricks, mouth dry and intolerably thirsty, plunged in God-forsaken darkness. That is the God for me! He laid aside His immunity to pain. He entered our world of flesh and blood, tears and death. He suffered for us. Our sufferings become more manageable in the light of His. There is still a question mark against human suffering, but over it we boldly stamp another mark, the cross that symbolizes divine suffering. The cross of Christ ... is God's only self-justification in such a world as ours." [14]

Jesus' identification with us in our suffering involved the whole spectrum of human sorrow: economic exploitation, political disenfranchisement, social ostracism, rejection and betrayal by friends, alienation from his own family, ridicule, humiliation, abandonment, beating, torture, despair, and, finally, a slow torturous death. Anyone who claims that God does not care about our suffering has not truly considered the implications of Christ's incarnation and death on the cross. The fact that God submitted Himself to such an extreme course of action infers that there was no other option open to Him. And if that is how deeply and profoundly God loves us, we can only surmise that God must have VERY good reasons for allowing suffering to continue in our world. We may never fully understand those reasons in this life, but we can be absolutely assured of His profound love for us, and, by looking at the cross, we can trust that His purposes and plans for us are good.

The question of God allowing suffering leads us inevitably to a discussion of Hell. That is the topic of the next chapter.

Reflection Questions

1. *What new insights have you gained from this chapter? Has this chapter changed any of your views?*

2. *What questions or challenges has this chapter raised for you?*

3. *What do you understand about the logical necessity of suffering? (You may need to re-read that section of this chapter).*

4. *Read the curse of the Fall in Genesis 3:14-19. How does this help to explain the existence of suffering in the natural world?*

5. *Read 1 Peter 1:6-7. How does suffering sometimes play a remedial role in the life of the Christian? Does God cause this suffering?*

6. *What do you understand about the providential necessity of suffering? (You may need to re-read that section of this chapter).*

7. *What do you understand about the eschatological necessity of suffering? (You may need to re-read that section of this chapter).*

8. *How does Job's experience provide further context for our understanding of suffering?*

9. *Read 2 Corinthians 4:16-18. With what perspective are we encouraged to view our sufferings? How should this help us?*

SEVEN

THE PROBLEM OF HELL

The Christian doctrine of Hell poses a serious stumbling block to many people in seeking to believe in God. How can a God of love torture people in Hell? How can such cruelty be the actions of a fair and merciful God? In particular, it is the seemingly disproportionate and vindictive over-reaction of God that many people struggle with.

A very close friend recounts a disturbing incident from his childhood:

"One night, when I was 12 years old, my father came home drunk (as he often did) and accused me of doing something that I had not done. I was innocent of the supposed misdemeanour, but he did not believe me. He took off his belt and began beating me, demanding that I confess. I continued to plead my inno-

cence, but the beating only intensified, with my father yelling at me to admit my wrong-doing. Eventually I could take no more, so I confessed to a crime that I had not committed. This only made my father angrier, and he continued to beat me as punishment for having "lied" to him originally. The welts and bruises from that beating only lasted a week or so, but my sense of outrage at this injustice lasted much longer. One of the factors that contributed to my sense of injustice was that the misdemeanour I was wrongly accused of, was of an extremely trivial nature and did not warrant anything close to such a severe beating."

The term, *"cruel and unusual punishment"* is used to describe punishment that is considered to be unacceptable due to its unwarranted severity. Condemnation of cruel and unusual punishment has been built into the constitutions of many western democracies, including the English Bill of Rights (1689), the Eighth Amendment to The United States Constitution (1791), the European Convention on Human Rights (1950) and the Universal Declaration of Human Rights adopted by the United Nations General Assembly (1948). As compassionate human beings, we insist that any discipline should be proportionate to the crime, with the aim of reforming the perpetrator rather than merely punishing, and we decry the use of arbitrary torture in any form.

It is this universal sense of justice and fairness that makes the Biblical doctrine of Hell so difficult to accept for many people. The torture of billions of people in the flames of Hell seems an extreme and disproportionate punishment; cruel and unusual indeed! Lee Strobel, the acclaimed investigative reporter who converted from atheism to Christianity, admits that this was a major stumbling block for him as he began to investigate the message of Christianity:

"...as a spiritual seeker, I found my sense of justice outraged by the Christian teaching about Hell...The doctrine seemed like cosmic overkill to me, an automatic and unappealable sentence to an eternity of torture and torment. It is mandatory sentencing taken to the extreme: everyone gets the same consequences, regardless of their circumstances. Step out of line with God— even a little bit, even inadvertently—and you're slapped with an endless prison sentence in a place that makes Leavenworth look like Disneyland."[1]

Before we go any further, it is important to point out that Christians are divided over the duration of God's punishment in Hell. There are two opposing viewpoints. The **perpetualist** view is that the souls of the unsaved will exist consciously and eternally in Hell, where they will be tormented forever. On the other hand, the **annihilationist** view is that the unsaved will be cast into the fires of Hell where they will be utterly destroyed, suffering briefly yet acutely in the process. My own views on this matter have changed dramatically in the course of writing this book. Both of these views, perpetualism and annihilationism, are examined in the next chapter, *"Eternal Torment or Total Destruction?"*. I have deliberately dealt with this issue separately, as it is a rather heavy topic, involving detailed exegesis of the many Bible passages proposed by both viewpoints in support of their arguments. Read it at your peril!

In the meantime, even if one believes that the unsaved will be utterly destroyed in the fires of Hell, and will not suffer eternally, does this completely answer the objections of many people regarding the seeming unfairness of Hell? It certainly addresses a large part of their concern: the apparent cruelty of such an extreme and disproportionate eternal punishment. But surely the same concern remains valid, on a reduced scale, regarding the temporary suffering that God will inflict upon the unsaved when He casts them into the flames of Hell, where they will be finally destroyed. Although their torment will not be eternal, it will certainly be severe. The question must be asked, therefore, is even this temporary torment warranted? Is it not also extreme and disproportionate? How can God possibly be justified in torturing the vast majority of humanity, even briefly, when many of them appear to have barely warranted a parking ticket in this life? Surely a compassionate God would simply leave those who will not inherit eternal life in their graves. Why does He have to resurrect the unsaved from the grave, only to torture and kill them again? Why does there have to be a Hell at all? In order to begin to make sense of this, we need to understand several foundational concepts.

HELL IS NOT GOD'S "DUMMY SPIT"!

Some abuse of children is the result of parents simply losing their temper. They snap, momentarily losing control of themselves and acting in extreme ways that they later come to regret. Is Hell like this? Is it an extreme over-reaction because God has lost His temper?

Not at all. Hell is not God's dummy-spit. He hasn't lost control of Himself. There are two Biblical concepts that indicate that God is in complete control of Himself regarding Hell; the storing up of His wrath and the preparation of Hell. While the Bible does speak of God's fury and wrath, it is a frighteningly measured, calculated fury that is patiently biding its time as God awaits His final judgment. In Romans 2:5, Paul warns some people that *"because of your unrepentant heart, you are storing up **wrath** against yourself for the Day of God's wrath, when His righteous judgment will be revealed."* Clearly, God is not yet fully acting upon His wrath, but is storing it up for future expression. That future expression will be truly frightening. In a prophetic description of God's future judgment, Revelation 14:10 says, *"They will drink the wine of God's **fury**, which has been poured undiluted into the cup of His **wrath**".* For this reason, Hebrews 10:31 says, *"It is a fearful thing to fall into the hands of the living God."*

God's wrath against sin is furious, but it is under control. He has not yet unleashed it, but, instead, is storing it up. While the Bible elsewhere indicates that God's wrath is already being revealed in our world in a limited sense (Rom 1:18), it seems that the fullest expression of it is being reserved for a future *"Day of God's wrath"* (Rom 6:17). Until then, God's righteous anger against all the sin in the world remains in check, awaiting its final expression when divine justice will be finally instituted, and all sin will be judged and punished. The most common word used for God's wrath in the New Testament is "orgē" (ὀργή), which has the underlying, contextual meaning, *"to grow ripe for something."* It denotes something that builds up gradually over a long period of time in a controlled manner. In speaking of the use of this Greek word, Bible scholar, Leon Morris, observes, *"The Biblical writers habitually use for "the divine wrath" a word which denotes not so much a sudden flaring up of passion which is soon over, as a strong and settled opposition to all that is evil arising out of God's very nature"*[2].

James Boice explains this concept further when he states;

"We find this understanding of the wrath of God in Romans. In this letter Paul refers to wrath ten times. But in each instance

the word he uses is "orgē", and his point is not that God is suddenly flailing out in petulant anger against something that has offended him momentarily, but rather that God's firm, fearsome hatred of all wickedness is building up and will one day result in the eternal condemnation of all who are not justified by Christ's righteousness."[3]

The adjunct to this is the Biblical description of Hell being *"prepared"* for its future use; *"Then He will say to those on His left, 'Depart from me, you who are cursed, into the eternal fire that has been prepared for the devil and his angels'"* (Matt 25:41). As God awaits the Day of His judgment, He is deliberately preparing a place of punishment for the devil and his demons, as well as all those who remain unsaved. This is a calculated, measured preparation, planned in advance. Hell is not a result of God losing His temper in a momentary fit of rage; He has been planning and preparing it for millennia!

RIGHTEOUS WRATH

One of our problems in understanding the wrath of God is our experience of human anger. When we hear the word *"wrath"* we immediately interpret it in terms of human capricious anger and self-serving temper. Many people have had similar childhood experiences to my friend's previous example, and associate wrath with abuse and injustice. We are uneasy with the idea of God being wrathful, thinking that it is somehow unworthy of God's character. For this reason, God's wrath is not readily spoken of by most Christians or commonly addressed from the pulpit. But the writers of the Bible had no such reluctance. J. I. Packer states, *"One of the most striking things about the Bible is the vigour with which both Testaments emphasise the reality and terror of God's wrath."*[4] Arthur W. Pink noted, *"A study of the concordance will show that there are more references in Scripture to the anger, fury, and wrath of God than there are to His love and tenderness"*[5]. In fact, God's wrath is portrayed in the Bible as one of His perfect virtues.

One of our problems in understanding the wrath of God is that our concept of wrath is sullied by our experience of unjust, human anger. Unfortunately, human anger is often less than noble, because it can be characterised by at least one of the following:

- Loss of control
- Self-centred bias – a sense that I have not been treated as I deserve to be
- Desire for retribution for its own sake
- Injustice
- Disproportionate punishment

This kind of anger is rightly condemned in the Bible as sinful:

2 Cor. 12:20 *"For I am afraid that when I come I may not find you as I want you to be, and you may not find me as you want me to be. I fear that there may be quarrelling, jealousy, outbursts of anger, factions, slander, gossip, arrogance and disorder."*

Eph. 4:31 *"Get rid of all bitterness, rage and anger, brawling and slander, along with every form of malice."*

Col. 3:8 *"But now you must rid yourselves of all such things as these: anger, rage, malice, slander, and filthy language from your lips."*

However, not all human anger is sinful. Human anger can

be noble and completely justified. The Biblical exhortation, *"In your anger, do not sin"* (Eph 4:26), assumes that it is possible to be angry without it being necessarily sinful; it assumes that anger may sometimes be justified. Righteous anger is most obvious when we become indignant on behalf of others, as we respond to perceived injustice perpetrated against those who are innocent or oppressed. Human anger is most problematic when it arises from my own hurt, but is potentially noble when we become angry on behalf of others. For example, in 1 Samuel 11:6, we read, *"When Saul heard their words, the Spirit of God came upon him in power, and he burned with anger."* In this instance, Saul had learned of a plan by a pagan nation to inflict shameful injuries upon the occupants of an Israelite town and thereby bring the name of God into disrepute. Saul displayed righteous anger on behalf of God and the people of that town, and this occurred when *"the Spirit of God came upon him in power"*. There are similar accounts of righteous anger throughout the Bible: David (2 Sam 12:7); the Psalmist (Psalm 199:53); Jeremiah (Jer 15:17); the Corinthian Christians (2 Cor 7:8-11).

The clearest example of righteous anger in the Bible is when Jesus drove the money changers out of the Temple in Jerusalem (John 2:13-22). The extent of Jesus' anger is evident in the way He overturned the tables of the money lenders and drove them out of the temple with a whip. It was a violent expression of fury! Yet it was also considered and measured. John 2:15 states that Jesus *"made a whip of cords"*. This is extraordinary! Upon witnessing how the outer courts of the Temple had been turned into a market place, Jesus did not immediately react. Instead He went away and made a whip, constructing it from cords that He carefully braided together.

Only when it was complete did He return to the temple and unleash His righteous anger upon the money changers. This was no knee-jerk loss of temper, but a deliberate, controlled expression of indignation.

The extreme anger of Jesus on this occasion had a twofold cause. Firstly, Jesus was incensed that the money changers had completely taken over the outer courts which were meant to be reserved for the Gentiles to worship God. Thus, the missional aspect of the temple had been compromised – there was no place left for the Gentiles to come and worship. Secondly, turning the Temple into a common market place was an insult to God, who had decreed that the Temple was to be a holy place, solely dedicated to worshipping Him alone. This is why John described Jesus' anger in this incident by quoting from Psalm 69:9, *"Zeal for Your house will consume me"*. Jesus was angry on behalf of God and the misplaced worshippers, not on behalf of Himself. It is significant that the only occasions when we see Jesus angry in the Bible are those where He is angry on behalf of God or others. In contrast, Jesus never once expressed anger or rage when He was being ridiculed, insulted or tortured. In this way, Jesus exemplifies the truth that anger is most likely to be righteous and justified when it arises on behalf of others, rather than in response to our own perceived ill-treatment.

Righteous anger **does** exist. In fact, there are times and circumstances that demand from us nothing less than righteous anger. The question has to be asked, therefore, on what basis is God righteously angry? And, even if God's anger is justifiable, how can such an extreme measure as a torturous Hell, however brief, be warranted? How is it not an over-reaction? The answer to these questions lies in understanding three vital concepts: the seriousness of sin, the holiness of God and the justice of God.

THE SERIOUSNESS OF SIN

2,000 years ago, a married couple lied to their church elders and to God, and they immediately dropped dead (Acts 4:34 – 5:10). Just a simple little lie!

Now, consider that last statement; *"Just a simple little lie"*. Therein lies our problem. We mere mortals have very little appreciation of the truly diabolical, evil nature of sin. We have become desensitised to it because we are surrounded by sin every day of our lives. We live in a world of sin, and a world of sin lives in us. Hebrews 3:13 warns, *"take care that you do not become hardened by the deceitfulness of sin"*, but that is precisely what has happened to us as a race. We are so profoundly inured to sin, that we can only perceive its evil in its most extreme expressions: murder, rape, violence, abuse, genocide. We are rightly repulsed by these heinous crimes, but fail to recognise the same sinuous infection coursing through our own veins and manifesting itself in only slightly more civilised symptoms.

A.W. Tozer comments;

"No one has ever overstated the seriousness of sin ... The virus of sin has entered my life stream. It has conditioned my mind; it has affected my judgment. But sin is more than a disease. It is a deformity of the spirit, an abnormality in that part of human nature which is most like God's." [6]

To help us understand the nature and seriousness of sin, let me take you back to the Garden of Eden, where it all began. A piece of forbidden fruit was eaten, in direct disobedience to the command of God. No big deal; just a simple little sin, a single piece of fruit (or two at the most). No murder. No genocide. No rape. Surely this slight infringement only warranted a rap over the knuckles and a brief talking to? But no. The devastating curse, declared to Adam and Eve by God in Genesis 3, reveals the extreme seriousness of their crime. All of life, including the ongoing functioning of the physical universe itself, was "cursed" (Gen 3:14). Death, disease, pain and suffering are now our lot, as a direct result of our sin.

How can this be? How can such a simple act of disobedience warrant such extreme punishment? Because it wasn't a simple act of disobedience. It was the creature turning against his Creator. It was an act of treason against the King of the universe. A. W. Tozer explains the treasonous nature of sin and its universal consequences;

"Sin is a capital crime as well. It is treason against the great God Almighty who made the heavens and the earth. Sin is a crime against the moral order of the universe. Each time a man or woman strikes against God's moral nature and kingdom, he or she acts against the moral government of the entire universe."[7]

Sin, in essence, is the dethroning of God in our hearts. It is the treasonous refusal to abide by His commands. It is saying to the King of the universe, *"You can't tell me what to do! Who made you King anyway? I didn't vote for you! I hereby declare myself to be King! You are dismissed!"*

You may not have consciously said that to God, but that is effectively what we all say to Him each time we disobey His commands; even "little" sins like lying. James 2:10 states, *"If you break the Law [God's commands] at just one point, you are guilty of breaking all of it."* In other words, there is really no such thing as a little sin; all sin is treason. God has a perfect moral code that the subjects of His Kingdom are meant to obey, and when we break any part of that code we have broken it in its entirety. John MacArthur explains, *"The law of God is not a series of detached injunctions or commands, but a basic unity that requires perfect love of Him and our neighbours. Although all sins are not equally damaging or heinous, they all shatter that unity and render men transgressors, much like hitting a window with a hammer at only one point will shatter and destroy the whole window."*[8] Our sin has shattered the code of perfect allegiance to our Sovereign.

Furthermore, we have not broken this code a mere handful of times. Our rebellion is not a trifling matter of a few incidental blunders, but an outrageous litany of continual betrayal. The sheer volume of our sin over a single lifetime is incalculable. But let us, for argument's sake, say that we only sin three times each day, bearing in mind that Jesus defined sin as not only the things we do (sins of commission) but also failing to do the good that we know we should (sins of omission), as well as the evil nature of our thought life (sins of the mind). On this basis three sins in one day would be a bare minimum; a lustful thought, a selfish action, a hurtful comment, turning a blind eye to a situation where I should have offered assistance or spoken up in someone's defence, a "small" lie, a slight exaggeration, joining in with a smutty joke, passing on gossip, an angry or resentful thought, a jealous thought. It would be a truly good person who managed to scrape through the day with only three transgressions of God's moral code. Yet three sins per day amounts to over 1,000 sins in a year, and accumulates to 70,000 transgressions or more in a lifetime! A criminal standing trial in a court of law, who was guilty of this number of crimes, would have no chance of procuring leniency by pointing to the record of his good behaviour, because such a record does not exist! He would be laughed out of court! In the same way, when each of us stand in the presence of the Judge at the end of our lives, the claim, *"I have lived a good life"*, will carry no substance. In fact, it is a preposterous claim that reveals complete ignorance of the extent of our rebellion. Our souls are not white with merely an occasional smudge; they are as black as soot. And while I may currently be able to discern a significant difference between the blackness of a murderer's soul and my own, when we all stand before the blinding light of God's holiness on the Day of Judgment, those differences will be revealed to be merely varying shades of black. Isaiah 64:6 tells us that in the light of God's pure holiness, *"all our righteous acts are like filthy rags"*.

Hell becomes significantly more understandable when we realise the nature and depth of our sin. Sin is treason – and not just an occasional blunder, but treason on a monumental scale. It is the continual repetition of the original treasonous act that profoundly damaged the universe, which we perpetuate in dozens of ways every day. And Hell is God's response to our treason. It is the permanent banishment from the King's presence of all who have rebelled against His rule – all those who have indicated on a daily basis that they do not wish to be part of His Kingdom. On that great and terrible Day of Judgment no one can profess innocence, *"for all have sinned and fall short of the glory of God"* (Rom 3:23).

THE NATURE OF GOD – HIS HOLINESS

Hell becomes even more understandable when we comprehend a little more about the nature of God Himself. The twin aspects of God's nature that pertain particularly to the topic of Hell are His holiness and His justice.

God is holy. Really holy. Perfectly holy. Blazingly, blindingly holy. His holiness is a pure, blazing fire that would utterly consume us in our present sinful state if we came face to face with Him.

Part of our difficulty in perceiving the depth and profundity of our sin, is that all we have to compare ourselves with is other sinners. When my life is evaluated in the light of the nightly news, I can easily reach the conclusion that I am a reasonably good person. But if I was to stand for just a moment in the presence of the Holy God, the searing light of His perfect holiness would reveal my sin in all its ugliness and ignominy. Isaiah had precisely this experience, and it completely undid him. He was given a vision of the blazingly holy God, and this is how he responded:

"Woe is me! For I am lost! I am a man of unclean lips, and I dwell in the midst of a people of unclean lips; for my eyes have seen the King, the LORD of hosts!" (Isaiah 6:5).

In the light of God's perfect holiness, Isaiah suddenly saw his sin for what it was, and he thought he was about to die. He is not the only Biblical character to have had this experience. In Genesis 33, Moses foolishly asked to see God; *"Show me your glory"* (v.18). It was a foolish request, firstly because God is the omnipresent, transcendent God, who is not limited to space and time. Jesus tells us that *"God is spirit"* (John 4:24); an incorporeal spiritual being, unencumbered by the limitations of a particular physical form. Secondly, it was foolish because, as God immediately replied, *"No one can see me and live"* (Gen 33:20). Any sinful human being who, even for the briefest moment, stood fully and completely in the presence of the perfectly Holy God would be utterly destroyed, just as an ice cube would instantly vaporise if it found itself in the heart of the sun. Nevertheless, God acquiesced to Moses' request by appearing in a limited physical form, a theophany, walking past as Moses hid his face in a cleft between two rocks. Only in this way was Moses able to survive the encounter, and even then, one must surmise that the manifestation granted to him was the merest shadow of God's holy presence.

In the New Testament, the Apostle John was granted a vision of the risen Christ, in all of His heavenly glory, and John's response was to fall down in a dead faint! In Revelation 1:17, John recounts, *"When I saw Him, I fell down as though dead."* This was the ancient term for fainting. John was so overwhelmed by the blazing holiness of Jesus that he lost consciousness! Of course, John only saw a vision; he was not literally in the physical presence of Jesus's glory, for if he had been, he would not have survived. Remember, also, that John had been the closest disciple to Jesus during His earthly ministry. For three years John had shared a deep friendship with Jesus, and yet, when he saw Jesus as He is now, glorified in Heaven, he was terrified! The Jesus that John saw was significantly transformed. He blazed with a blinding, fierce light and emanated a truly terrifying holiness; *"His eyes were like blazing fire. His feet were like bronze glowing in a furnace, and His voice was like the sound of thunderous waters... coming out of His mouth was a sharp double-edged sword. His face was like the sun shining in all its brilliance."* (Rev 1:14-16).

Similarly, Saul, the persecutor of first century Christians, was struck blind when he encountered the blazing light of Christ's ascended glory while travelling to Damascus to arrest more Christians. Thankfully, Saul did not encounter the full, manifest presence of the ascended Christ, otherwise he, too, would have perished. He merely saw a *"light from heaven"* and a heard the voice of Christ (Acts 9:3), but it was enough strike terror into his heart and rob his eyes of sight.

The writer to the Hebrews writes of the blazing holiness of God; *"let us be thankful, and so worship God acceptably with reverence and awe, for our God is a **consuming fire**"* (Heb 12:28-29). We need to understand the devastating purity of God's holiness. It is a purity that will one day consume all sin. The fact that sin and sinners will be utterly destroyed on the Day of Judgment is not merely a wrathful act of divine punishment, but is the inevitable consequence of sinners coming fully and finally into the presence of the consuming fire of God's holiness.

THE NATURE OF GOD – HIS JUSTICE

The adjunct to God's holiness is His justice. God's justice **demands** that sin be punished.

Many of us remember the shocking murder, in 2013, of Reeva Steenkamp, who was shot to death by her boyfriend, Oscar Pistorius, when he fired four bullets through the bathroom door, behind which she was cowering. What was particularly shocking was that the court initially dismissed the charge of murder and convicted Pistorius of the lesser crime of culpable homicide, resulting in him only serving 10 months in prison before being released into house detention. The international outcry at this injustice was overwhelming. The world's press was dumbfounded. Reeva Steenkamp's family were outraged, as was anyone who had a moral conscience. The South African prosecutors who worked on the case described the sentence as *"shockingly lenient"*. Thankfully, justice prevailed in the end. An appeal by the state prosecutors resulted in Pistorius being convicted of murder and sent to prison for 15 years.

Even in our fallen, imperfect world, humans rightly perceive that evil must not go unpunished. We demand justice; we insist that perpetrators be brought to trial and made to pay for their crimes. If a judge goes soft on crime, issuing grossly inadequate sentences or failing to convict someone who is obviously guilty, society rises up in righteous indignation and demands that justice be carried out.

The Bible declares that God is a God of justice who will not allow wrong-doing to go unpunished. The Psalmist writes, *"For I, the Lord, love justice"* (Psalm 61:8). The Apostle Paul declares, *"God will repay each person according to what they have done"* (Romans 2:6). Moses expressed the same truth when he wrote, *"the Lord will not let the guilty go unpunished"* (Exod 34:7). Furthermore, God's judgment of every person will be perfectly fair. He will not make mistakes and cannot be influenced or swayed; *"God is a righteous judge"* (Psalm 7:11).

Hell is the ultimate expression of God's righteous judgment against mankind's cosmic treason. It is the means by which God will implement full and final justice. Sin will not go unpunished. Evil will not be overlooked. To those who accuse God of inaction against evil, of turning a blind eye to all the horrors and injustices of this world, the Bible declares that there will, indeed, come a Day of reckoning, when all evil will be exposed and punished in the fury of God's wrath. If you are ever tempted to think that God is complacent about the evil that is perpetrated day by day in His world, you only need to read again the Biblical descriptions of the coming wrath of God on the Day of Judgment, to have that notion overturned. God hates sin and has promised to deal with it in the most severe fashion. John Murray describes God's wrath by saying, *"Wrath is the holy revulsion of God's being against that which is the contradiction of his holiness."*[9]

In one sense, this is good news. It assures us that although some wicked people may seem to "get away with it" in this life, they will eventually get what they deserve. Evil dictators and perpetrators of genocide will suffer the full force of God's fury. Murderers, rapists and child molesters, though they may evade the clutches of the law in this life, will not evade the ultimate punishment that is due to them for their evil. For such people, the fires of Hell seem entirely appropriate. One would not accuse God of over-reacting when he raises Adolf Hitler and Pol Pot from the grave, only to throw them into the Lake of Fire where they will burn in agony as they are destroyed – their souls eternally obliterated from the universe. This would seem a just punishment for monsters who have murdered millions of innocent people.

The problem, of course, is that God's justice will not only be executed upon the worst sinners, but upon all sinners. None of us will escape His justice. All who have sinned will be cast into the same fire, unless they have accepted His offer of clemency and responded in faith and repentance to Christ. All sin and all sinners will meet the same fate. All of us are guilty of cosmic treason on a monumental scale, and the difference between the best and worst of sinners is negligible when compared to the towering holiness of God. Imagine standing at the top of the highest skyscraper and looking down at two ants on the pavement below. Though one ant may be ten times the size of the other, in comparison to the height of the skyscraper their difference is insignificant. The height of **both** ants is laughably incomparable to the height of the skyscraper. The same is true when the relative virtue of each person is measured against the towering holiness of God. *"All have sinned and **fall short** of the glory of God"* (Rom 3:23). We are all **so far** short of God's perfect standard that none of us can rightly complain that God's severe justice is undeserved.

Hell becomes completely understandable if we properly comprehend the seriousness of sin and the holiness and justice of God. Indeed, these truths cry out for some kind of final reckoning. God's perfect **justice** is such that He cannot, and will not, allow evil to go unpunished. Every instance of disobedience to God's perfect moral code will be punished. God's perfect **holiness** is such that sin cannot remain in His presence. Sin and sinners can no more survive in His presence than an ice cube can survive in the heart of the sun. Hell represents the blazing fire of God's holiness and justice, finally extinguishing every trace of evil from the universe.

These truths become more confronting when we consider our own dire predicament as profound sinners. Over the course of our lives, each one of us is guilty of an incalculable number of breaches of God's moral standards, each of which individually constitutes an act of cosmic treason – rebellion against God's right to tell us how we ought to live. And each of these instances is a capital offense, punishable by death.

The cross of Jesus represents God's ultimate solution to our predicament, satisfying God's justice and holiness, and providing the means by which clemency can be offered. By punishing Jesus in our place, God offers complete forgiveness to all who will turn to Christ in faith and repentance. Chapter

13 of this book will examine the atonement of Christ, not only in this light, but also as the ultimate context for our understanding of Hell.

Reflection Questions

1. What new insights have you gained from this chapter? Has this chapter changed any of your views?

2. What questions or challenges has this chapter raised for you?

3. Read Romans 2:5-6. How comfortable are you with the concept of God being wrathful?

4. Read John 2:13-22. Are you comfortable with Jesus' display of anger in this incident? What made Him so angry?

5. Do you think it is possible for humans to be righteously angry? Under what circumstances?

6. Read Genesis 33:18-20 and Hebrews 12:28-29. Why is God described as a "consuming fire"? What should our response be?

7. Read Romans 2:6 and Revelation 20:13. Do these verses leave open any possibility of accusing God of unfairness or harshness?

8. How should we respond to the twin concepts of the holiness and justice of God?

EIGHT

ETERNAL TORMENT OR TOTAL DESTRUCTION?

WARNING: This is chapter deals with issues that are doctrinally heavy! It explores the question of whether the Bible actually teaches that people will be tormented in Hell **eternally**, or whether Hell will be the means of their utter **annihilation**. In order to assess these two opposing views, this chapter explores a large number of Bible passages at depth. If you find detailed Biblical exegesis dull, or you are not interested in this topic, feel free to skip this chapter. If, however, you are one of those people who have always struggled with the concept of God torturing people for eternity, read on! I invite you, in fact I challenge you, to re-investigate the teaching of the Bible, to see if it really does teach the concept of eternal torture.

The traditional Christian teaching of Hell as a place of

eternal torment seems an extreme and disproportionate punishment, and one that many people have struggled to come to terms with. Acclaimed Christian author, Lee Strobel, admits that this was a major obstacle for him as he began to investigate the message of Christianity[1]. Similarly, C.S. Lewis expressed his great unease at the prospect of God torturing people for eternity;

"There is no doctrine I would more willingly remove from Christianity than (Hell), if it lay in my power. We are told that it is a detestable doctrine and, indeed, I too detest it from the bottom of my heart."[2]

Theologian, Dr. Samuele Bacchiocchi, in his book, "Immortality or Resurrection?"[3], provides a poignant summary of the concerns that many people have:

"Few teachings have troubled the human conscience over the centuries more than the Traditional view of Hell as the place where the lost suffer conscious punishment in body and soul for all eternity. The prospect that one day a vast number of people will be consigned to the everlasting torment of Hell is most disturbing and distressing to sensitive Christians. After all, almost everyone has friends or family members who have died without making a commitment to Christ. The prospect of one day seeing them agonizing in Hell for all eternity can easily lead thinking people to say to God: 'No thank you God. I am not interested in your kind of paradise!'"

It is not surprising that the traditional view of Hell as a place of eternal torment has been a stumbling block for believers and an effective weapon used by sceptics to challenge the credibility of the Christian message. But is this view of Hell Biblical? Does the Bible actually teach this view? Ultimately, this is the only question that matters. Our particular unease with the concept of eternal torment is not grounds for dismissing it. We cannot, indeed must not, seek to reinterpret the Bible simply to alleviate our discomfit or dilute doctrines that we find distasteful. Our quest is for the Truth, even if it entails concepts that are puzzling or disturbing.

For many years I accepted the traditional view of Hell as a place of eternal torment, taught to me by people I respected. Recently, however, I have re-examined the Scriptures. I have spent long hours poring over the many texts used to support this traditional view of Hell, examining the lexical, literary and immediate context of each passage, and I have come to an extraordinary conclusion; the concept of eternal torment in Hell is not supported by sound exegesis of the Scriptures. In fact, at certain points, it arises from a fundamental disregard of some foundational hermeneutic principles.

It is important to acknowledge, however, that greater minds than ours continue to disagree on this subject. There are still many respected Bible teachers who cling to the perpetualist view; the view that souls are tormented perpetually in an eternal Hell. J.I. Packer, for example, continues to argue strongly for Hell as a place of eternal torment. On the other hand, a growing number of respected scholars, such as John Stott, Michael Green and Clark Pinnock are convinced of the Biblical basis for the annihilationist view; that the unsaved will be cast into Hell at the final judgment, where they will suffer the flames of God's wrath as their souls are finally and completely destroyed. This view is also referred to as Conditional Immortality; that only the saved will live forever.

The ongoing debate over this doctrine indicates the complexity of the topic and the lack of unequivocal clarity in the Scriptures concerning the issue. While this should urge caution and humility upon us, it should not paralyse us. Each of us have the responsibility to search the Scriptures for ourselves, in order to refine our theology, so that our *"love may abound more and more in **knowledge** and depth of **insight**"* (Phil 1:9).

Scriptural Evidence For Annihilation Of The Unsaved

THE VOCABULARY OF DESTRUCTION

One of the major problems with the perpetualist view of Hell (that Hell is a place of eternal torment), is the many references to people being "destroyed" in Hell. The Bible consistently applies the vocabulary of destruction to the unsaved:

PSALM 1:6

"The Lord watches over the way of the righteous, but the way of the wicked will be destroyed."

PSALM 92:7

"Though the wicked spring up like grass and evildoers flourish, they will be destroyed forever."

The claim that these and other verses refer to an eternal process of destruction, one which is ongoing and is never completed, does not appear to be the simplest and clearest interpretation. The Hebrew word for *"destroyed"* here is "shamad" (שָׁמַד), which, according to all standard Hebrew / Greek lexicons, means, *"to exterminate or annihilate"*[4]. Shamad is used 90 times in the Old Testament, and in each instance, it indisputably infers complete annihilation. It is simply not possible to interpret these verses in Psalms to mean anything other than complete and total destruction. The addition of the word *"forever"* in Psalm 95 (*"destroyed forever"*), simply indicates that the destruction of the unsaved will be permanent – it will last forever and will never be reversed.

MATTHEW 10:28

"Do not be afraid of those who kill the body but cannot kill the soul. Rather, be afraid of the One who can destroy both soul and body in Hell."

This is an extremely important verse for our understanding of the nature of Hell. The two separate sentences within this verse are a form of parallelism, where the second is in contrast to the first. The first sentence tells us that there are some who *"can kill the body but cannot kill the soul"*. The second provides the contrast, by declaring that God, on the other hand, **can** kill both body and soul when He *"destroy[s] both soul and body in Hell."* Surely, this verse cannot be any clearer! The Greek word for *"destroy"* here is apolesai (ἀπολέσαι), from its derivative, apollumi (ἀπόλλυμι), which literally means *"to kill, destroy or cause to perish"*[5]. It indicates a very final end to those who are cast into Hell.

This word, apollumi, is used regularly in the New Testament to refer to killing. For example:

- In Matthew 2:13, Herod wants to *kill* the baby Jesus.
- In Matthew 12:14 the Pharisees conspired together about how they might *kill* Jesus.

- In Matthew 21:41 (story of the wicked tenants) the vineyard owner *kills* the wicked tenants.
- In Matthew 27:20, the elders and chief priests urge the people to have Barabbas released and Jesus *killed*.
- In Mark 3:6, the Pharisees plot to *kill* Jesus.
- In Mark 9:22, the parents of a boy with an unclean spirit tell Jesus that the spirit often throws the boy into water or into a fire, trying to *kill* him.

Perpetualists argue that apollumi can sometimes also mean *"ruin or spoil"*, thereby arguing that Matthew 10:28 is declaring that the souls of the unsaved will be perpetually tormented and ruined, rather than completely annihilated. It is true that the word can sometimes have this meaning, in the same way that our English word, *"destroyed"*, can be used metaphorically; for example, *"we destroyed the opposition today"*. However, whenever a word has two possible meanings, we are not at liberty to arbitrarily choose the meaning that best suits our purposes. Rigorous hermeneutics requires that we determine the intended meaning from the context of the passage itself. In the case of Matthew 10:28, the context leaves us in no doubt as to the intended meaning. The parallelism of this verse demands that we interpret the phrases *"kill the soul"* in the first sentence and *"destroy both soul and body"* in the second, to be speaking of exactly the same thing – the complete and utter destruction of both body and soul in Hell. Interpreting this verse in any other way requires an extreme disregard of basic hermeneutics (the accepted principles of Biblical interpretation). It is the blatant disregard of these simple principles which renders the perpetualist interpretation of this verse untenable. This statement by Jesus in Matthew 10:28 is unequivocal, and represents the Achilles heel of the perpetualist argument.

JOHN 3:16

"*God so loved the world that He gave His only Son, that whoever believes in Him should not perish but have everlasting life.*"

The Greek word translated here as "*perish*" is apoletai (ἀπόληται), from the same derivative, apollumi, (ἀπόλλυμι - "*destroy*"). Once again, this is not referring to eternal torture; it is contrastive with "*eternal life*". This is not merely a contrast between a happy eternal life and an agonising eternal life; it is a more fundamental contrast between those who will live forever and those who will not.

ROMANS 6:23

"*For the wages of sin is death, but the gift of God is eternal life in Christ Jesus our Lord.*"

The Greek word for death, here, is θάνατος (thanatos). It literally means death, complete annihilation, and it is used 106 times in the New Testament to mean precisely that! The wages of sin is not eternal torture. Once again there is a stark contrast being made between those who will live forever and those who will not.

JAMES 4:12

"*There is only one Lawgiver and Judge, who is able to save and to destroy.*"

James is speaking of the Day of Judgment when Christ will exercise His right to save some and destroy others. Once again, the word "apollumi" (to utterly "*destroy*"), is used. This verse completely negates any sense of the unsaved existing eternally.

PHILIPPIANS 3:18-19

"*There are many who live as enemies of the cross of Christ. Their destiny is destruction.*"

The is the exactly the same word (apollumi), and exactly the same concept.

2 THESSALONIANS 1:6-10

" *⁶ God is just: He will pay back trouble to those who trouble you ⁷ and give relief to you who are troubled, and to us as well. This will happen when the Lord Jesus is revealed from heaven in blazing fire with His powerful angels. ⁸ He will punish those who do not know God and do not obey the gospel of our Lord Jesus. ⁹ They will be punished with everlasting destruction [apollumi] and shut out [cut off] from the presence of the Lord and from the glory of His might ¹⁰ on the day He comes to be glorified in His holy people and to be marvelled at among all those who have believed.*"

This is the same concept of everlasting destruction that was referred to in Psalm 92. Once again, the use of the adjective "*everlasting*" does not refer to a **process** of destruction that lasts forever, but the fact that the destruction of the unsaved is **permanent** and irreversible; they will be annihilated for all eternity, never to be raised to life again. Because of this, they will be unable to enter God's paradise; they will be *"shut out from the presence of the Lord"*. Some perpetualists have tried to argue that the fact that the unsaved are *"shut out from the presence of the Lord"* infers conscious existence, requiring God to essentially lock the door to heaven to keep them out. But what more complete way of being cut off from God than being a non-existent soul? Surely this is an equally reasonable explanation of how these people are cut off from God? Either of these interpretations of being *"shut out / cut off"* from God's presence is valid and reasonable. Which are we to embrace? Once again, whenever there are two possible interpretations of a verse, we must let the immediate context guide us, rather than our predetermined preference. In this case, the preceding half of the verse has already indicated that the unsaved will be destroyed, hence the second interpretation is the intended one.

HEBREWS 10:39

"But we do not belong to those who shrink back and are destroyed [apollumi], but to those who have faith and are saved." Once again, the contrast between being destroyed and being saved is stark.

John Stott, the revered evangelical theologian and Bible scholar, comments about the New Testament's consistent use of the word "apollumi" (*"destroyed"*) to describe the eventual fate of the unsaved:

"It would seem strange...if people who are said to suffer destruction are in fact not destroyed; and...it is difficult to imagine a perpetually inconclusive process of perishing."[6]

It is this repeated use of the word "destroyed" in scripture that poses the greatest problem for the perpetualist's argument.

THE SECOND DEATH

Another significant passage for our understanding of the fate of the unsaved, is Revelation 20:12-15:

" *¹² And I saw the dead, great and small, standing before the throne, and books were opened. Another book was opened, which is the Book of Life. The dead were judged according to what they had done as recorded in the books. ¹³ The sea gave up the dead that were in it, and death and Hades gave up the dead that were in them, and each person was judged according to what they had done. ¹⁴ Then death and Hades were thrown into the lake of fire. The lake of fire is the second death.¹⁵ Anyone whose name was not found written in the Book of Life was thrown into the lake of fire."*

This passage describes the resurrection of all people at the end of history to stand before the judgment seat of Christ. The casting of the unsaved into the lake of fire (Hell) is referred to here as the second death. This is a crucial concept. The first death is temporary, because it will be followed by the resurrection and judgement. The second death is permanent. The first death involves the destruction of only the body. In the second death, both body and soul will be destroyed. The second death cannot simply mean eternal torment, because it is intrinsically linked to the first. They are both *"deaths"* in the absolute sense; a first death and a second death. To be consistent we cannot interpret the first death literally and the second death metaphorically – this would defy all accepted hermeneutical principles! The second death must be interpreted in the context of the previously mentioned New Testament passages which describe the *"destruction"* of the unsaved.

CONDITIONAL IMMORTALITY

A popular belief among Christians is that the human soul is inherently immortal, and that this necessitates eternal existence in either Heaven or Hell. This concept of the universal immortality of the human soul was first developed by Plato and his fellow Greek philosophers. Their postulating regarding the indestructibility of the human soul profoundly influenced early Christian speculation about the after-life. The popular doctrine that has since developed within Christian circles, that all human souls are essentially immortal as a consequence of mankind's creation in the image of God, and therefore that all souls will necessarily exist eternally beyond the grave, owes a great deal to these ancient philosophers. Bible scholar, F.F. Bruce comments, *"It is a truism that Plato's teaching [on the immortality of the soul] has profoundly influenced Christian anthropology."*[7] When we turn to the Bible, however, the evidence for the inherent immortality of the human soul is simply not there. On the contrary, several key passages negate this concept.

Genesis 3 indicates that mankind forfeited the chance of immortality in the Garden of Eden, requiring God to take preventative measures to ensure that we did not subsequently live forever in our fallen state:

"[22] And the Lord God said, "The man has now become like one of us, knowing good and evil. He must not be allowed to reach out his hand and take also from the tree of life and eat, and live forever."[23] So the Lord God banished him from the Garden

of Eden to work the ground from which he had been taken. ²⁴ After He drove the man out, He placed on the east side of the Garden of Eden cherubim and a flaming sword flashing back and forth to guard the way to the tree of life."

This foundational passage unequivocally declares that God has undertaken steps to ensure that unsaved people will not live forever! Human beings are not inherently immortal.

Subsequent to mankind's Fall, immortality is only available through the grace of Christ, to those who respond to Him in faith and repentance:

"To those who by persistence in doing good seek glory, honour and immortality, He will give eternal life." (Romans 2:7)

"I am the living bread who came down from heaven. If anyone eats of this bread, he will live forever." (John 6:51)

"He [Jesus], has destroyed death and has brought life and immortality to light through the gospel." (2 Timothy 1:9b-10)

The concept that only those who respond to Christ will live forever is known as Conditional Immortality, and is the adjunct to the doctrine of Annihilation (that all who are outside of Christ will be destroyed at the final judgment).

SCRIPTURES THAT ARE COMMONLY CITED TO SUPPORT ETERNAL TORMENT OF THE SOUL

LUKE 16:19-31

In this parable of the rich man and Lazarus, Jesus portrays

the condemned, deceased, rich man as being conscious and *"in agony in these flames"* (v. 24). This is a passage often cited by perpetualists as evidence of eternal torment in Hell. However, there are several fundamental flaws in their argument. Firstly, the rich man is in **Hades**, not Hell. Hades (Ἅιδης) is the New Testament term for the Old Testament concept of Sheol (שְׁאוֹל), and is the temporary abode of the unsaved prior to the Day of Judgment when they will be cast into Hell and destroyed. Revelation 20, previously examined, indicates that *"death and Hades gave up the dead that were in them"* (v.13) at the future resurrection and that once all judgment has been completed, Hades will be *"thrown into the lake of fire"* (v.14). The parable of the rich man and Lazarus indicates that at least some of the unsaved dead, as they await the future Day of Judgment, will be in torment, already experiencing a taste of God's wrath. This, however, will not last forever, but will conclude with their eventual public condemnation at the end of history and their destruction in the fires of Hell. This is further evidenced by the reference in the parable to the rich man's brothers who are still living and whom he wishes to warn. Clearly, this story is set in the intermediate period between the first death and the second death, while life on earth continues. While the parable is intriguing for the possible insights it provides as to the state of the lost as they await their final judgment, it has nothing to tell us about Hell.

MATTHEW 25:41

"Then He will say to those on His left, 'Depart from me, you who are cursed, into the <u>eternal fire</u> prepared for the devil and his angels.'"

Jesus also uses a similar description of Hell as a place of eternal fire in Matthew 18:8. The text in both cases indicates that it is the fire that burns eternally, not those who are thrown into it. The eternal nature of the flames indicates the complete ability of the fire to consume and utterly destroy those thrown into it; the fire won't expire with the job half done! The eternal nature of the flames also serves as a perpetual reminder of the fierce justice of a Holy God. But there is nothing in this verse to indicate that the unsaved will survive eternally in those flames.

MATTHEW 8:12

"They will be thrown into the outer darkness where there will be weeping and gnashing of teeth."

This is a very popular proof text used by perpetualists to substantiate the concept of eternal torment in Hell. However, it overlooks several key interpretative points. **Firstly**, and at a very simple level, there is nothing in the verse that indicates that the weeping and gnashing of teeth will continue forever. The assertion that the suffering of the unsaved will last forever is an assumption that has no basis in this text. This passage simply reveals that those who are thrown into Hell will be in great distress as they are consumed by the fires of God's wrath. There is nothing in this verse that contradicts the annihilationist view of suffering in Hell as the unsaved are being destroyed.

Secondly, gnashing of teeth was a first century cultural expression of anger and hatred, rather than an expression of pain and suffering. For example, In Acts 7:54, the Jewish Sanhedrin *"gnashed their teeth"* at Stephen as they stoned him to death. Similarly, Psalm 37:12 says, *"The wicked plot against* *the righteous and gnash their teeth at them"*. Rather than describing the suffering of the unsaved at this point, Jesus is specifically referring to the fact that the unsaved will continue to express defiance and resentment towards God, even as they are being destroyed in the fury of His wrath.

Thirdly, the *"outer darkness"* is not a contradiction of Hell as a place of fire; it merely indicates that Hell is a place completely removed from the light of God's presence.

MATTHEW 25:46

"Then they will go away to eternal punishment, but the righteous to eternal life"

Perpetualists argue that if the word *"eternal"* (*aionios* [αἰώνιος]) is used for both the reward of the righteous and the punishment of the wicked, the duration must be the same. However, a distinction must be made between the punishing and the punishment. The punishment of the unsaved is, indeed, eternal, because they will be destroyed, never to rise again, and never to take part in God's eternal Kingdom. Their punishment is eternal in its outcome. They are not "sin-binned" out of the game for a few thousand years and may re-enter once they have served their time. They are excluded forever. Their destruction is permanent. The act of punishing, however, only lasts for as long as it takes for the unsaved to be consumed in the fires of Hell. Distinguishing between a noun of action and its associated verb (punishment versus punish) enables us to understand that this verse is referring to the everlasting outcome of the finite act of punishing.[8]

. . .

MARK 9:48

"...thrown into Hell [Gehenna] where the worm does not die and the fire is not quenched"

This is another verse often cited to substantiate eternal, conscious torment in Hell. The argument used by perpetualists is that the unsaved are supposedly never completely consumed by both the worms (maggots) and the fire. What is often overlooked, however, is that Jesus is quoting from Isaiah 66:24, which explicitly states that the worms and fire are doing their work upon the **corpses** of God's enemies, not upon living beings; *"And they will go out and look on the dead bodies of those who rebelled against me; the worms that eat them will not die, the fire that burns them will not be quenched, and they will be loathsome to all mankind."* Those being burned and eaten are already dead! The insistence of both these passages that the worm will not die and the fire will not be extinguished in no way indicates eternal existence of the unsaved. It simply implies that the unsaved will be completely consumed; there is no chance of the flames being extinguished or the worms ceasing their work and leaving them only half consumed. This passage actually supports the annihilationist view of the complete destruction of the unsaved rather than the perpetualist view of eternal suffering.

JUDE 13

"... for whom the gloom of utter darkness has been reserved forever"

This is the Biblical pronouncement of punishment that is reserved for false teachers. Perpetualists claim that this infers eternal, conscious existence in a state of gloomy banishment.

Significantly, verse 7 of this passage in Jude indicates that their punishment is also eternal fire, as befell the people of Sodom and Gomorrah; *"In the same way, Sodom and Gomorrah and the surrounding towns gave themselves up to sexual immorality and perversion. They serve as an example of those who suffer the punishment of eternal fire."* Jude is making the point that those who perpetuate false teaching will suffer the same fate as the people of Sodom and Gomorrah in the Old Testament. The people of Sodom and Gomorrah were completely destroyed! This helps us to contextualise the *"utter darkness"* of verse 13. This is the darkness of oblivion; of complete annihilation. The Bible elsewhere uses the imagery of darkness to indicate oblivion. In Job 3:3-10, for example, Job expresses the desire that he had never been born, saying of his birthday, *"Let that day be darkness! May ... light not shine upon it. Let gloom and deep darkness claim it."* Job is not speaking of the darkness of conscious existence here, but rather, the darkness of non-existence. When understood in both its immediate context and its literary context, Jude 13 actually supports annihilationism rather than perpetualism.

REVELATION 14:9-11

"They will be tormented with burning sulphur in the presence of the holy angels and of the Lamb. And the smoke of their torment will rise forever and ever. There will be no rest, day or night, for those who worship the beast and its image."

Without doubt, this is one of the major arrows in the perpetualist's quiver. Nevertheless, it ignores the crucial fact that these verses are part of a warning of the impending judgement about to be visited upon God's enemies, which is then immediately followed by a description of the actual judgement, several verses later, in Rev. 14:14-20. The actual description of this final judgement is a vivid, gruesome picture of utter death and destruction, not of endless torment. Gods enemies are *"gathered like clusters of grapes"* (v.18) and thrown *"into the great winepress of God's wrath"* (v.19) where they are crushed to death, resulting in blood flowing out of the press and *"rising as high as a horse's bridle for a distance of 300 kilometres"* (v.20). We look in vain in this passage to find a picture of eternal, conscious torment. There is torment, certainly, but it ends in the complete obliteration of the enemies of God. In this context, the statement in verse 11, about there being no rest for God's enemies, is simply the prophetic description of them being hunted down and destroyed by God's avenging angels in the verses that follow. Additionally, the statement, *"the smoke of their torment will rise forever and ever"*, is imagery taken straight from Isaiah 34:8-10, which describes the fires which completely destroyed the city of Edom, where God also decreed that *"its smoke shall go up forever"*. Clearly the city of Edom is not still burning, it was completely destroyed long ago, along with its occupants. There is no actual smoke still rising. Nor are the citizens of Edom still in torment; they were annihilated millennia ago! The smoke rising up forever is a metaphor indicating the perpetual **memory** of God's judgment upon the wicked, as a lasting testimony to His justice and righteous wrath. This passage makes an important distinction between the finite act of judgement and its perpetual memory; the unsaved will be utterly and completely destroyed, but the memory of God's just judgment upon them will remain in perpetuity.

. . .

REVELATION 20:10

"And the devil, who deceived them, was thrown into the lake of burning sulphur, where the beast and the false prophet had been thrown. They will be tormented day and night for ever and ever."

The specific revelation given, here, to the Apostle John, is that the devil and his evil spiritual accomplices will be tormented eternally; there is no destruction for them. We are not told the reason for this. Perhaps it is because of some inherent difference in their created natures, when compared to mortal humanity. More likely, it is due to the just judgment of God that has determined that the depth of their evil warrants eternal punishment.

Whatever the explanation, however, we must not paint humanity with the same brush. We cannot assume that the same fate must befall all who are thrown into the lake of fire, for this would contradict the clear teaching of Scripture elsewhere regarding the complete destruction of the unsaved. In verse 14, we are told that when the unsaved are consigned to the lake of fire it will be their "**second death**" – a term we have already seen as referring to complete annihilation. The unsaved will perish in fire, no doubt with great with torment, but ultimately, they will cease to exist.

Some annihilationists have difficulty with the concept of the devil's eternal torment, and interpret this reference as metaphorical. I am unconvinced by this interpretation, as there are no contextual indicators within the passage that point to a metaphorical meaning. Nor can we explain this reference as mere apocalyptic imagery. The statement, *"They will be tormented day and night for ever and ever"* is a clear propositional truth. Attempts to explain it as metaphorical arise more from presuppositional bias than from scholarly exegesis.

The traditional perpetualist view of eternal torment in Hell appears to be grounded in poor exegesis of several key passages. The most common exegetical error has been the failure to engage with contextual issues. Often the immediate, literary context of a passage completely contradicts the perpetualist interpretation. At other times, when words have two possible meanings, perpetualists have chosen the one that suits their purposes, rather than being guided by contextual considerations.

Scripture does not support the concept of eternal torment in Hell. Those outside of Christ will be raised to life with all humanity to face God's judgment. The unsaved will stand before their Creator, be condemned for their sins, and suffer the flames of Hell until they are utterly consumed.[9]

Reflection Questions

1. What new insights have you gained from this chapter? Has this chapter changed your view of the duration of Hell?

2. What questions or challenges has this chapter raised for you?

3. Has the concept of eternal torture in Hell been a stumbling block for you or for someone you know?

4. Read Matthew 10:26-28. What is verse 26 talking about?

5. In verse 28, what is the clear inference regarding the duration of the soul's existence in Hell?

6. Read John 3:16. There is a clear juxtaposition in this well-known verse between those who are saved and those who are not. What is that juxtaposition?

7. Read Revelation 20:12-15. Why do you think that the Bible refers to the lake of fire (Hell) as the "second death"? What is the clear inference of this statement?

8. Read Psalm 92:7. What is the clearest, simplest interpretation of this statement?

9. What Bible passages still trouble you regarding the possibility of perpetual torment in Hell? How do you respond to the explanations provided in this chapter?

NINE

SET UP TO FAIL?

During a recent email correspondence on the topic of God's existence, an earnest seeker expressed what I consider to be a significant objection:

"*I don't see how it can be fair for God to create something (everyone alive today), and then tell the thing you created that they deserve a horrible punishment for being the way they were made. To put it another way, God has made standards that we can't meet, and then condemns us for not meeting them. So, every single person deserves Hell, simply for being human. If every single human being that has ever lived would have done the same thing [as Adam and Eve], what does that say about humans? Why is He punishing His creations for being the way they were created?*"

Many would agree with this objection, claiming that it is grossly unjust that God should punish humanity for sin when we are incapable of not sinning. Many would claim that we were effectively "set up" to fail. They would ask why God punishes us for an inherent flaw that He allowed in the first place. What response can be made to this objection?

IN THE BEGINNING

We must start by distinguishing between creation and causality. God created us with free wills, but He did not cause us to misuse them; we did that on our own. Our misuse of a good gift of God cannot be blamed on the giver. This is not an entirely satisfactory answer, however, because the sceptic could argue that God's giving of free will to mankind was akin to a parent giving a child a loaded gun to play with and then blaming the child when he shoots himself. This argument has a small degree of merit, because God certainly knew that He was giving us a dangerous gift. In fact, because God is omniscient (all-knowing), He knew with absolute certainty that we would misuse our free will to rebel against Him. But this does not make God the cause of our sin and evil. The analogy of giving a child a loaded gun breaks down at a couple of key points.

Firstly, unlike the case of the child with the gun, Adam and Eve were adults with high order brain function, arguably with significantly greater mental acuity than we currently possess in our fallen state. They were fully cognisant that they were disobeying God; they were aware that they were misusing their free wills to rebel against their Creator. Their rebellion was not an accident with a loaded gun, but a deliberate choice.

Secondly, a loaded gun has only one purpose; to inflict

harm. In giving such a dangerous weapon to a child it is inevitable that nothing good will eventuate. Our free wills, however, have potential for both good and harm. Had we used our free wills as we were instructed to, and for the purpose for which they were intended, great good would have eventuated. True love and obedience would have ensued, attended by the full complement of eternal blessings that God had prepared for us.

Thirdly, we were explicitly warned against disobedience, with the disastrous consequences clearly articulated; *"You must not eat from the tree of the knowledge of good and evil, for when you eat from it you will certainly die."* (Gen 2:17).

In each of these respects, God is without blame. We cannot point the finger at Him and say, *"It's your fault! You made me like this!"* However, we are still only scratching the surface, because the sceptic will point out that if God is omniscient, then He foresaw our misuse of free will but still chose to create us with free wills anyway. Therefore, the sceptic claims that the blame must, ultimately, rest with God.

The claim of God's ultimate culpability in our rebellion can only be justified if it can be shown that the free will that He instilled within us was inherently flawed; that it had a predetermined bias towards rebellion which we were powerless to oppose. Yet this is not the case at all. We must not assume that Adam and Eve's free wills resembled our own currently flawed ones. Our current inbuilt bias towards sin was not created by God, but is a congenitally inherited spiritual disease which sprang into being at the moment of our ancestors' insidious rebellion. We must not confuse God's foreknowledge with deliberate pre-programming. He did not predispose us to sin. He simply knew in advance that this would be the outcome. Sceptics might argue that God's foreknowledge must surely render Him culpable for all the evil and suffering that has since ensued, since He went ahead with our creation anyway.

Several things must be said at this point.

Firstly, there appear to have been only three logical choices facing God at the beginning of creation. To create us with free wills, to create us as robots incapable of disobedience, or to not create us at all. That God chose the former is hardly surprising, since no sane person would prefer robotic existence or complete non-existence over our current condition. God, it appears, feels the same way. A robotic humanity would not be capable of giving or receiving love, and God is a God of love.

Secondly, we have already discussed in a previous chapter the logical impossibility of free will existing without the possibility of it being misused for evil. Free will essentially carries with it the potential for both good and evil. We cannot demand of God, *"Why didn't you give us free wills that were incapable of disobedience?"*, for such a notion is self-contradictory.

Thirdly, God's omniscient foreknowledge of the misuse of our free wills and the terrible suffering that would ensue, was not a matter of indifference to Him. He did not create us and then step aside, saying *"Oh dear, this is going to get very messy, but it's not my concern."* Rather, the Bible indicates that God had already planned His rescue mission before the first humans drew breath. The Apostle Peter refers to this extraordinary pre-historic redemption plan when he states, *"You were redeemed from the empty way of life handed down to you from your ancestors, with the precious blood of Christ, a lamb without blemish or defect. He was chosen before the* *creation of the world, but was revealed in these last times for your sake"* (1 Peter 1:18-20).

This is a truly mind-boggling concept. God foresaw the terrible consequences of our misuse of free will, and had already determined that Jesus would need to die on the cross to redeem us – and this was *"before the creation of the world"*! That such a drastic course of action had already been pre-planned from eternity reveals that the catastrophic consequences of free will were providentially and logically unavoidable. It also must surely exonerate God from any culpability for our own deliberate evil. At our creation, God was effectively saying, *"I will give you the precious gift of self-determination. I will bestow upon you the gift of free will, knowing that you will misuse it. And then I will give you an even greater gift: I will one day die to redeem you, so that some of you may freely choose to accept my forgiveness and live with me in the love and light of eternity."* Such a God of love can in no way be held accountable for the wickedness of our rebellion. The potential for human love to be freely given was so highly valued by God, that He was prepared to pay a double cost: the introduction of suffering into His perfect creation, and the death of His Son to redeem fallen mankind.

THE NATURE OF OUR NATURE

We have established the fact that before we were even created, God knew that we would rebel. Yet we cannot lay the blame for our rebellion at His feet. God did not create our predisposition for sin; we did that ourselves. At this point, a sceptic might argue, *"I accept that God didn't create us with a sinful bias, but the result is that every human being now has that bias. How is it fair that God punishes us for our sin when we are completely incapable of not sinning?"*

On the surface, this objection seems to have some merit. If God is still demanding perfection, yet this is now an impossibility for us, isn't there a case for claiming that His expectations are too high and the punishment of Hell too severe? How can we be blamed for sin when it is a natural bias that is hard-wired into us? Punishing us for sin makes as much sense as a lawn bowler who becomes angry with his bowls because they don't travel in a straight line!

It is certainly true that all human beings are incapable of living a sinless life. As 1 Kings 8:46 states, *"There is no one who does not sin."* This is because we are all infected with a sinful nature, inherited from our progenitors, Adam and Eve. The Apostle Paul writes, *"Therefore, just as sin entered the world through one man, and death through sin, and in this way, death came to all people, because all sinned ... one trespass resulted in condemnation for all people ... through the disobedience of the one man the many were made sinners"* (Rom 5:12,18). In these few verses of Romans, Paul explains a deeply disturbing truth; every human being who has been born subsequent to Adam and Eve has inherited from them a congenital spiritual deformity of the soul; a darkness of the heart that draws us inevitably towards sin. This is often referred to as "**original sin**"; the sinful tendencies, desires, and dispositions in our hearts with which we are all born. Original sin is the perpetual tragedy of every new baby being born with an already morally ruined character, one that will unfailingly result in the habitual committing of sin. In Romans 7, Paul explains that we are all now slaves to our sinful natures, unable to consistently resist our dark urges:

"I am unspiritual, sold as a slave to sin. I do not understand what I do. For what I want to do, I do not do, but what I hate I do.... I know that good does not live in me, that is, in my sinful nature. For I have the desire to do what is good, but I cannot carry it out. I do not do the good I want to do, but the evil I do not want to do—this I keep on doing." (Rom 7:14-19).

But the situation is graver than this. It is not simply a case that we have a powerful sinful nature that predisposes us to sin. We sin because we are already sinners. Psalm 51 describes the fact that we are not merely born with a tendency to sin, we are already sinners at birth. King David states, *"Surely I was sinful at birth, sinful from the time my mother conceived me."* (Psalm 51:5). This is because the sin of Adam and Eve has been **imputed** to each one of us, as if we were the ones who committed the original act of treason. The Apostle Paul refers to this when he points out that we were all *"in Adam"* when he sinned (1 Cor 15:21). In Romans 5:13 Paul uses the word "imputed" to talk about the judicial passing on of guilt from one to many, and then a few verses later, spells this out more fully when he explains that *"through the disobedience of the one man the many were made sinners"* (Rom 5:18). In simple terms, the Bible indicates that every human being is now deemed to be guilty of Adam's sin. Evangelical author and theologian, Matt Perman, explains:

"The guilt of Adam's sin is credited not just to Adam himself, but to us all. We are regarded as having sinned in Adam, and hence as deserving of the same punishment. This is imputed sin. Thus, we not only receive polluted and sinful natures because of Adam's sin (original sin), but we are also regarded as having sinned in Adam such that we are guilty of his act as well (imputed sin). Imputed sin is the ruin of our stand-

ing before God and is thus not an internal quality but an objective reckoning of guilt, whereas original sin is the ruin of our character and thus is a reference to internal qualities. Both original sin and imputed sin place us under the judgment of God."[1]

How can the guilt of one man be imputed to the whole of humanity? How is this fair? It must be conceded that not all Christians interpret Romans 5 to be referring to the imputation of Adam's guilt to all mankind. The precise meaning of Paul's phrasing in key sections of Romans 5 leaves open the alternate possible explanation that it is only Adam's sinful nature that is passed on to us, not the guilt of his particular sin.[2] This view, however, does not account for the much clearer wording of Psalm 51:5, which requires hyperbolic interpretation in order to dismiss its seemingly clear message; *"Surely I was sinful at birth, sinful from the time my mother conceived me."* On balance, the concept of imputation of Adam's guilt seems substantiated.

Of course, none of this helps us in responding to the sceptic's claim that God is unfair for punishing us for something that (a) somebody else did, and (b) we can't help doing now. In fact, this understanding of original sin and imputed sin seems to bolster their case! This is where we need to understand the Biblical concept of individual culpability.

CULPABILITY

Our culpability operates at two levels: federal culpability and personal culpability.

. . .

Federal Culpability

Scripture gives no comprehensive explanation of the judicial reasoning behind the imputation of Adam's guilt to all mankind. However, Paul's comment that we were *"in Adam"* (1 Cor 15:21) together with his statements in Romans 5 have led theologians to postulate that, in a spiritual sense, the whole of humanity was seminally present within Adam when he sinned. Furthermore, it is widely proposed that the only way that universal imputation would be fair is if God knew that every human being would have made the same choice had any of us been present instead of Adam. In this sense, Adam was a fair federal representative, and God is completely just in condemning us all. In other words, I am entirely culpable for Adam's sin, and God is justified in condemning me for that first sin, because He knows that I would have acted in precisely the same manner. Some theologians take the concept even further, suggesting that each one of us actually <u>did</u> commit Adam's sin along with him, because we were seminally present within him in a metaphysical sense.

The concept of federal culpability, however, becomes a completely moot point once we consider the implications of our ongoing personal culpability. As we shall now see, there is more than enough culpability there to convict each of us for eternity!

Personal Culpability

Despite the fact that we have a sinful nature which gives us a predisposed bias towards sin, the Bible is clear that sin is always a choice. Paul's pronouncement in Romans 7 that we are slaves to our sinful nature, refers to the cumulative inevitability that we will all sin, together with the impossibility of remaining sinless throughout our lives. It does not, however, predicate that at every point of temptation in my life I must, inevitably, sin. Our own experience confirms this; we have all successfully resisted temptation. In fact, we do this all the time by exercising restraint and maintaining self-control. Although it is inevitable that we will sometimes give in to our sinful natures in moments of weakness, at which point *"what [we] want to do [we] do not do"* (Rom 7:14), yet at each moment of our lives we retain the ability to resist temptation through a deliberate choice of our wills. If this was not the case, our world would be utterly and chaotically evil, with each of us continually giving full reign to our lust, greed and avarice.

The Bible regularly assumes our ability to resist temptation:

- *"In your anger, do not sin"* (Ephesians 4:26)
- *"No temptation has overtaken you except what is common to mankind. And God is faithful; He will not let you be tempted beyond what you can bear. But when you are tempted, He will also provide a way out so that you can endure it."* (1 Cor 10:13)
- *"Throw off everything that hinders and the sin that so easily entangles."* (Heb 12:1)
- *"Resist the devil and he will flee from you"* (James 4:7)

Similarly, the Scriptures are replete with exhortations for people to *"repent"* (Matt 4:17; Luke 13:3; Acts 2:38). This infers that people who are currently living in sinful rebellion to God have the capacity to choose, by an act of their will, to cease their sinfulness and submit to Him. The fact that most people do not make this choice is not due to absolute powerlessness in the face of their overwhelming sinful nature, but to their own unwillingness. They simply do not want to stop sinning. God's looming judgment, therefore, is not an unfair penalty imposed upon helpless victims, but the deserved consequence for people who have failed to exercise self-control and resist their sinful urges. Ultimately, people are culpable because they choose to sin.

This is not the only aspect of our personal culpability. People are also culpable for refusing to accept Christ as Lord and Saviour, and, ultimately, it is this refusal that will separate them from God eternally. A sacrifice for sin has been made, through the death of Christ on the cross. His crucifixion was the atoning sacrifice for the sins of the world, and His resurrection was confirmation of the efficacy of that sacrifice. An offer of forgiveness has been made; a free pardon for all who will turn to Him in faith and repentance. There remains no reason for anyone to suffer God's wrath for their sins; no reason except their own, stubborn, hard-hearted refusal to repent. It is sadly ironic that, without exception, every person who has ever complained to me about God's harshness or unfairness in punishing sin, has been someone who is refusing His offer of forgiveness. It is akin to a death row prisoner who is offered a free pardon but refuses to accept it, and then complains as he is being led to the electric chair!

"In the past God overlooked such ignorance, but now He commands all people everywhere to repent. For He has set a day when He will judge the world with justice by the man He has appointed. He has given proof of this to everyone by raising Him from the dead." (Acts 17:30-31).

Reflection Questions

1. What new insights have you gained from this chapter? Has this chapter changed any of your views?

2. What questions or challenges has this chapter raised for you?

3. Read 1 Peter 1:18-20. This is a truly mind-boggling concept. What is it saying? Explain.

4. Read Genesis 2;17. In what sense did we "die" when we ate from the tree of the knowledge of good and evil?

5. Read Romans 5:12-18 and Psalm 51:5. What is your understanding of "original sin" and "imputed sin". (You may need to re-read that section of this chapter).

6. Read Romans 7:14-19. If we are incapable of not sinning, how is it fair that God still punishes us?

7. Read 1 Corinthians 10:13. What does this verse, together with the Bible's regular exhortation for people to "repent" (eg. Acts 2:38), infer about people's personal culpability?

8. How should we respond to a sceptic who says that God is unfair for punishing us for an inbuilt bias that we are all born with?

9. Read Acts 17:30-31. How should this verse influence us as we seek to share our faith with those who do not yet know the Lord?

TEN

LOVE ME, OR ELSE!

God demands that we love Him. Jesus indicated that the greatest and most important of all the commandments is to *"love the Lord your God with all your heart, all your strength, all your soul and all your mind"* (Matt 22:37), which is a quote from Deuteronomy 6:5. God does not merely ask us to love Him; He commands it. Those who refuse to love Him will one day be banished into the fires of Hell. Can you already see the objection forming on the lips of sceptics? Can you sense their outrage rising? In case you can't, their objection goes something like this:

"*What kind of despotic, narcissistic God creates us and demands that we love Him, then tortures those who refuse?*

What sort of insecurity must He have that He cannot tolerate people not loving him?"

At a less colloquial level, the essence of this objection is that God needs our love in order to be fulfilled or whole; that without our love He is somehow deficient or incomplete. The argument continues that, if this is so, then surely it contradicts the very definition of God; for God, by definition, must be self-sufficient. Objections by sceptics go further still. If, as Christians claim, the universe was created by God to display His glory, is this not also egotism on a grand scale? And does it not also indicate a deficiency within God – that He needed to create the universe in order to achieve a sense of completeness? These are profound questions, that go to very heart of the nature of God and the origin of the universe.

THE ASEITY OF GOD

Aseity is a theological term that refers to the self-existence and self-sufficiency of God. However else we might interpret God's command that we love Him, it cannot contradict either the self-existence or self-sufficiency of God. But firstly, let us be clear regarding the meaning of these concepts.

God is the only "thing" in the universe that is self-existent. He exists from within Himself; He is self-generating. Everything else in the universe is dependent and derived. Humans, for example, are not self-existent. We require food, warmth, oxygen, gravity, and the whole gamut of natural laws and universal constants in order to exist. The very essence of our life force comes not from the material world or from within us, but from God *"in whom we live and move and have our being"* (Acts 17:28). Even matter, the very stuff of the universe, is not self-existent. It requires the continued operation of the 28 universal constants (fundamental laws of nature) in order to exist. If the empirical strength of any one of these constants was altered by even one millionth of a degree, life as we know it would be impossible and, in the case of many of the constants, matter would simply cease to exist; electrons would lose their orbital attraction to the nuclei and atoms would fly apart.

The following table lists (again) the precisely tuned universal constants that govern our physical universe:

Table of Universal Constants[1]

Quantity	Symbol	Numerical value	Unit
Acceleration of free fall (standard)	g_0	9.8066	m/s^2
Atmospheric pressure (standard)	p_0	1.0132×10^5	Pa
Atomic mass unit	u	1.6606×10^{-27}	kg
Avogadro constant	N_A	6.0220×10^{23}	mol^{-1}
Bohr magneton	μ_B	9.2741×10^{-24}	J/T, $A m^2$
Boltzmann constant	k	1.3807×10^{-23}	J/K
Electron			
charge	$-e$	1.6022×10^{-19}	C
mass	m_e	9.1095×10^{-31}	kg
charge/mass ratio	e/m_e	1.7588×10^{11}	C/kg
Faraday constant	F	9.6485×10^4	C/mol
Free space			
electric constant	ε_0	8.8542×10^{-12}	F/m
intrinsic impedance	Z_0	376.7	Ω
magnetic constant	μ_0	$4\pi \times 10^{-7}$	H/m
speed of electromagnetic waves	c	2.9979×10^8	m/s
Gravitational constant	G	6.6732×10^{-11}	$N m^2/kg^2$
Ideal molar gas constant	R	8.3144	J/(mol K)
Molar volume at s.t.p.	V_m	2.2414×10^{-2}	m^3/mol
Neutron rest mass	m_n	1.6748×10^{-27}	kg
Planck constant	h	6.6262×10^{-34}	Js
normalised	$h/2\pi$	1.0546×10^{-34}	Js
Proton			
charge	$+e$	1.6022×10^{-19}	C
rest mass	m_p	1.6726×10^{-27}	kg
charge/mass ratio	e/m_p	0.9579×10^8	C/kg
Radiation constants	c_1	3.7418×10^{-16}	$W m^2$
	c_2	1.4388×10^{-2}	m K
Rydberg constant	R_H	1.0968×10^7	m^{-1}
Stefan-Boltzmann constant	σ	5.6703×10^{-8}	$J/(m^2 K^4)$
Wien constant	k_w	2.8978×10^{-3}	m K

Even these universal constants, themselves, are not self-existent. They do not exist necessarily. They do not cause themselves to exist, but are caused by Someone Else. It is the

Triune God (the Trinity) who creates and upholds the universal laws and constants:

"For in Him [Christ] all things were created, things in heaven and on earth, visible and invisible, whether thrones or dominions or rulers or authorities. All things were created through Him and for Him. He is before / above / over all things, and in Him all things hold together." (Col 1:16-17)

It is Christ who *"holds together"* the very matter of the universe and upholds the universal constants. The "laws of nature" are not really laws of nature at all; they are the laws of God. They are the ongoing means by which God holds the universe together and ensures its reliably proper functioning. Undergirding the very existence of our physical universe is a metaphysical, transcendent God; a God who exists above and beyond nature itself. If this transcendent God completely withdrew His presence from our universe for even one second, it would simply fall apart and cease to exist. The universe is not self-existent.

But God is not like anything else in the universe. He is self-existent. He is uncaused. He exists necessarily. His existence does not require or depend upon anything or anyone else. He simply is. The triune God is the only being who has life within Himself; *"For as the Father has life in himself, so he has granted the Son also to have life in himself."* (John 5:26). If there was no universe, no matter, no gravity, no anything, God would still exist. In fact, He did exist like this for eternity past, before the creation of the world. His existence is eternally underived, hence His revelation to Moses of His name; *"I am who I am"* (Exod 3:14). This is not merely the utterance of an enigmatic name, but the proclamation of God's timeless and self-generating nature. He exists eternally in the present, and the source of that existence is Himself. Jesus used the same reference to describe His own eternal self-existence, when He said, *"Truly, truly, I say to you, before Abraham was, I am"* (John 8:58). Similarly, the Psalmist declares, *"Before the mountains were born or You gave birth to the earth and the world, even from everlasting to everlasting, You are God"* (Psalm 90:2).

Not only is God self-existent, He is also self-sufficient. This means that there is nothing lacking within Him that needs anything or anyone else in order to be complete or made whole. In particular, human love and praise is not necessary for God. We are not necessary for His wholeness or completeness. In fact, God does not need anything, other than Himself:

"The God who made the world and everything in it is the Lord of heaven and earth and does not live in temples built by human hands.[25] *And He is not served by human hands, <u>as if He needed anything</u>. Rather, He himself gives everyone life and breath and everything else.*[26] *From one man He made all the nations, that they should inhabit the whole earth; and He marked out their appointed times in history and the boundaries of their lands.*[27] *God did this so that they would seek Him and perhaps reach out for Him and find Him, though He is not far from any one of us.*[28] *'For in Him we live and move and have our being'."* (Acts 17:24-28)

Verse 25 (above) could not be clearer: God does not need **anything**. He does not need our praise. He does not need our love. He is not deficient in self-worth, thereby requiring re-affirmation, nor does He have a rampant ego requiring constant praise. He did not create us because He was lonely, nor did He create the universe because He was bored. He is completely and perfectly self-contained and self-sufficient.

This self-sufficiency is intrinsically tied to His triune

nature. The transcendent Creator is ONE God, but He is not a singularity as humans are singularities. The consubstantial Trinity, Father, Son and Holy Spirit - one substance but three entities - enjoyed perfect love, harmony and fellowship within Himself for eternity past. Jesus spoke of this during His earthly existence when He said, *"And now, Father, glorify me in Your presence with the glory I had with You before the world began"* (John 17:5). Later in that same chapter Jesus refers to *"Your love for me before the foundation of the world."* (John 17:24). Mere human minds cannot conceptualise this eternal self-sufficiency within the Trinity; a perpetual state of internal love, harmony and joy that was and is so perfect that nothing could possibly add to it or diminish it.

This is what is meant by God's eternal self-sufficiency; and this is why any suggestion that God needs the love of weak, insignificant human beings is laughable. Hence, the Psalmist declares; *"What is mankind that you are mindful of them, human beings that you care for them?"* (Psalm 8:4). This does not infer that God does not love us (for He surely does), but that He does not need us. The aseity of God is such that He is in need of nothing.

THE REASON FOR CREATION

Why then did God create the universe? If He was already perfectly self-sufficient, why did He bother to create anything at all? John Piper explains;

"In creation, God 'went public' with the glory that reverberates joyfully between the Father and the Son. There is something about the fullness of God's joy that inclines it to overflow. There is an expansive quality to His joy. It wants to share itself. The

impulse to create the world was not from weakness, as though God were lacking in some perfection that creation could supply."[2]

A fountain overflows not because it has a need to do so, but simply because that is its nature. Or, as Jonathon Edwards famously stated, *"Tis no argument of the emptiness or deficiency of a fountain that it is inclined to overflow."*[3] God's nature is to create and to love. It does not flow out of a need or a deficiency within Him, but from an overflow of His already perfect self-sufficiency. The physical universe was created by God to display His greatness and glory to mankind; *"The heavens declare the glory of God, the stars proclaim the work of His hands."* (Psalm 19:1). The universe, it its infinite greatness and mid-boggling beauty is God's masterpiece that declares to mankind, *"This is a glimpse of what I am like"*.

Mankind was also created for God's glory. In Isaiah 43:6, the Lord states, *"Bring my sons from afar and my daughters from the end of the earth, everyone who is called by my Name, whom I created for my glory, whom I formed and made."* Our ultimate purpose is to glorify God. And not only is this our purpose, but also that of the heavenly beings as well. In Revelation 4, The Apostle John is given a glimpse into the throne room of heaven, where he sees *"four living creatures"* at the foot of God's throne, who *"day and night, never stop saying, 'Holy, holy, holy, is the Lord God Almighty, who was, and is, and is to come'."* (Rev 4:8). In the same scene, John also witnesses *"twenty-four elders"* who constantly *"fall down before Him who sits on the throne"* and say, *"You are worthy, our Lord and God, to receive glory and honour and power, for You created all things, and by Your will they were created and have their being"* (Rev 4:9-11).

The universe, and every being within it, was created to glorify God. Yet we are only scratching the surface of the issue at this point. Creation has a deeper, more profound purpose. The whole universe was created in order, ultimately, for God to be glorified through the death and resurrection of His Son, Jesus Christ. This is a vital concept to grasp. God's rescue mission through Christ was not an after-thought, a "Plan B" after things went sour. It was always God's "Plan A". The physical universe is God's purpose-built stage for the appearance of His Son, through whose atoning sacrifice to redeem a lost humanity, God would be glorified. Ephesians 1 tells us that this was planned before the creation of the world, and assures Christians that *"God chose us in Him before the foundation of the world. He predestined us for adoption as sons through Jesus Christ to the praise of the glory of His grace"* (Ephesians 1:4-6). Paul refers to this eternal plan of God elsewhere; *"He has saved us and called us to a holy life—not because of anything we have done but because of His own purpose and grace. This grace was given us in Christ Jesus before the beginning of time, but it has now been revealed through the appearing of our Saviour, Christ"* (2 Tim 1:9-10). Our messed up, fallen world, and God's need to intervene in the most drastic and costly manner, is not a mistake. It was meant to be. It was planned from eternity.

John Piper explains, with his usual alacrity:

"Why did God create the world? ... God created the world for His glory. God did not create out of need. He did not create the world out of a deficiency that needed to be made up. He was not lonely. He was supremely happy in the fellowship of the Trinity — Father, Son, and Holy Spirit. He created the world to put His glory on display that His people might know Him, and love Him, and show Him. And why did He create a world that would

become like this world — a world that fell into sin, a world that exchanged His glory for the glory of images? Why would He permit and guide and sustain such a world? ... For the praise of the glory of the grace of God displayed supremely in the death of Jesus."[4]

IS GOD THE ULTIMATE EGOTIST?

However, this still does not answer the charge of narcissistic egotism, levelled against God by sceptics. Even the great C. S. Lewis admitted that one of the obstacles he had to overcome as he began to explore the Christian faith was the constant demand from God *"for our worship like a vain woman who wants compliments."*[5] I suspect that many Christians are slightly uncomfortable with God's constant concern for His own glory. Consider this passage where God spoke through the prophet Ezekiel to the Israelites;

"Thus says the Lord God: It is not for your sake, O house of Israel, that I am about to act, but for the sake of my holy Name, which you have profaned among the nations to which you came. And I will vindicate the holiness of my great Name, which has been profaned among the nations, and which you have profaned among them. And the nations will know that I am the Lord, declares the Lord God, when through you I vindicate my holiness before their eyes" [Ezekiel 36:22-23].

In this passage, God is stating that the reason He is about to intervene in Israel's plight, is not for their sake, but for the glory of His own name. He appears more concerned for His reputation than He is for the welfare of the Israelites! In fact, throughout the Bible's narrative, God is continually seeking to glorify His name:

- *"Bring my sons from afar and my daughters from the end of the earth, everyone who is called by my Name, whom I created for my glory."* (Isaiah 43:6-7)
- *"I made the whole house of Israel and the whole house of Judah cling to me, says the Lord, that they might be for me a people, a name, a praise, and a glory."* (Jeremiah 13:11)
- *"Our fathers rebelled against the Most High at the Red Sea. Yet he saved them for His Name's sake that He might make known His power."* (Psalm 106:7-8)
- *"For my Names sake I defer my anger, for the sake of my praise I restrain it for you. . . . For my own sake, for my own sake I do it, for how should my Name be profaned? My glory I will not give to another."* (Isaiah 48:9-11)
- *"He comes on that day to be glorified in His saints and to be marvelled at in all who have believed."* (2 Thessalonians 1:9-10)

Here is an interesting thought: Christians have no problem believing that they should be God-centred, but they are a little uncomfortable about God being so God-centred. Why is that? I suggest it is due to two factors, the same two factors that lie behind the sceptics claim of God's supposed egotism; anthropomorphism and an inadequate view of God's perfection.

ANTHROPOMORPHISM

When people accuse God of egotism, megalomania or narcissism, they are anthropomorphising Him. They are attributing to God unworthy motives and attitudes that are endemic within humanity. Human tyrants crave adulation, and egotists prop up their self-esteem by creating and maintaining a false image of themselves to the world. When people seek to exalt themselves and seek glory for themselves, we rightly condemn this. We regard egotism and self-aggrandisement as an ugly side of human nature because it seeks to raise one's self up and be seen to be better than others.

The reason why this sort of behaviour often provokes a strong reaction from discerning people is that we know that those who are acting in this way are no better than anyone else. Pop stars who strut around as if they are gods still wake up every morning with bad breath and need to use the bathroom. They are weak, imperfect creatures, just as we all are, and this is all too often revealed in the way their worlds eventually fall apart. We see pop stars who are ravaged by drug addiction and depression. We see football stars with alcohol addiction who beat up their wives and girlfriends. We see movie stars who leave behind a trail of failed marriages and broken relationships. The suicide rates amongst these so called "stars" is horrendous. The unthinking masses may fall for their pageantry, and worship mindlessly at their feet, but those of us with more than a few synapses firing see their egotism for the fraud that it is. Their self-aggrandisement is ugly and contemptible, and we rightly denounce it. To those who prance around, effectively saying, *"Look at me! Aren't I great?"*, the thinking populace silently responds, *"No you're not. You're no better than me, and I refuse to bow down to you."* Egotism is ugly because it is false. It is doubly ugly because it almost always involves putting others down so that the egotist can be raised up.

This is our experience of the ugliness of human egotism. Sadly, it is this human context that we sometimes bring to God's claim of greatness. When God declares, *"Look at me! I am great! I am Holy! I am worthy of your worship!"*, our entrenched response is to treat this with the same disdain with which we have treated all previous claims of greatness. We immediately assign to God the same twisted motives that we have seen in despots, tyrants, megalomaniacs and pathetic egotists throughout human history. Why should God be any different?

Why indeed...

THE PERFECTION OF GOD

The transformative truth that we must come to terms with is that God is the one Being in the universe who is completely and utterly worthy of our worship. God is perfect in a way that we cannot even begin to conceptualise. He is perfect in His unlimited power. He is perfect in His knowledge and wisdom. He is perfect in His goodness and holiness. He is perfect in love. He is perfect in His judgment of sin. He is perfectly and completely present in every molecule of the universe. He sees all, and knows all, and holds the entire created universe in the palm of His hand.

This is the perfect God who says to us, *"I am the only One who is worthy of your worship. There is no other."* We are right to denounce other claims to greatness as egotistical nonsense, but we are utter fools if we seek to do the same with our Creator. To accuse God of hubris is akin to a single-celled amoeba standing up to Einstein and saying, *"Who do you think you are? You're nothing special!"*

The God who calls us to worship Him is the One who carved the Grand Canyon and shaped the Himalayas, who sculped the icecaps and scooped out the ocean depths, who spoke billions of galaxies into existence with the power of His voice. To refuse to worship such a Creator and, even more unthinkable, to even question His right to be worshipped, displays a level of ignorance and arrogance that is truly appalling.

THE RESTORATIVE NATURE OF GOD'S GLORY

Another reason we should not confuse God's desire for glorification with ugly human egotism, is that God's motivation is entirely different. God desires to be glorified, not so that He may feel better about Himself, but so that creature and Creator may be in their right relationship. For when people are on their knees before the God who made them, they are in the very place they were created to be, and will discover that it brings with it an experience of profound joy and fulfillment. In demanding that people worship and glorify Him, God is not imposing an arbitrary, selfish demand upon us. He is requiring that we humbly acknowledge the absolute truth of His greatness. As often and as genuinely as we do this, we divest ourselves of the arrogance and rebellious pride that has been the downfall of the human race since the dawn of time, and we re-enter the glorious, joyful relationship with our Maker that we lost in the Garden of Eden. God's call to worship and glorify Him is a call to repentance and restoration; a call to re-discovered joy and fulfilment. Egotism seeks to exalt self at the expense of others. God's desire to be glorified is so that all of creation may be restored to its perfect, former balance; *"to bring unity to all things in heaven and on the earth under Christ."* (Eph 1:10).

WHY DOES GOD PUNISH THOSE WHO DO NOT GLORIFY HIM?

God's punishment of those who refuse to glorify Him is not the capricious tantrum of a megalomaniac whose fragile ego has been offended. Rather, it is the just action of a righteous judge. Those who refuse to worship God perpetuate the original act of rebellion in the Garden of Eden. They effectively say, *"Who made you King? I didn't vote for you!"* God is completely just in banishing these people from His eternal Kingdom, because they have effectively excluded themselves. And for those who might claim that they did not know about God, He has declared that there is no excuse for failing to glorify Him, for He has made His existence abundantly clear:

"His invisible attributes, namely, his eternal power and divine nature, have been clearly perceived, ever since the creation of the world, in the things that have been made. So people are without excuse. For although they knew God, they did not glorify Him as God." (Romans 1:20–21)

Even worse than ignoring the clear evidence that God has left, people's rejection of God is an insult to the cross of Christ. God has done everything possible to reach out and redeem a lost humanity, culminating in the death of Christ on the cross. For those who ignore even this, there remains no alternative but to face God's judgment and be banished from His presence for eternity.

God alone is worthy of our worship. Choosing to love, obey and worship Him places us exactly where we belong and restores the right relationship which were created to enjoy.

Reflection Questions

1. What new insights have you gained from this chapter? Has this chapter changed any of your views?

2. What questions or challenges has this chapter raised for you?

3. Read Matthew 22:37. Is God egotistical for demanding that people love Him? Why or why not?

4. What do you understand about the aseity of God? (You may need to re-read that section of this chapter).

5. Read John 5:26 and John 8:58. What does this reveal about the nature of God?

6. Read Acts 17:24-28. Does God need anything? Does He need our love? Why or why not?

7. Read Colossians 1:16-17. What profound truths does this passage reveal about Christ and His relationship to the universe? In what sense does Christ "hold all things together"?

8. Read John 17:5 and 24. What do these verses reveal about the nature of the Trinity?

9. Read Isaiah 43:6. What is the ultimate purpose of mankind?

10. How would you respond to a sceptic who claims that God is an egotist for demanding that we love Him?

ELEVEN

CHRISTIANS BEHAVING BADLY

A significant speed bump in some people's quest to find God is the abhorrent behaviour of some who claim to be Christians. Perhaps you have been turned away from Christianity by such people, yourself. You may have encountered people who claim to be Christians, but whose lives contradict the profession of their faith. There are people who claim to be Christians who have affairs, who are greedy and dishonest, who lie and cheat and steal, who have bitter hearts and poisonous tongues. Even worse, some so-called Christians commit the most heinous crimes, including sexual abuse and paedophilia. In recent decades, media reports and various investigations have brought to light many examples of this kind of appallingly sick behaviour amongst both laity and clergy, and I suspect that this is one of the factors that has led to the wholesale rejection of religion by a large and growing percentage of people within Western society. There are many people who feel disillusioned and betrayed by religion because of this kind of seemingly endemic behaviour. In order to respond to this issue, let me start by telling you a story.

For many years, my wife and I were staunch supporters of our regional football (soccer) team, the Central Coast Mariners. We were paid-up platinum members of the club, with reserved seats in the grandstand. At one of the first home games we ever attended, there was some very poor behaviour amongst a small group of Mariners supporters in the grandstand on the far side of the ground. They were obviously intoxicated and were abusing the nearby opposition supporters, using obscene language and throwing beer at them. After the match, as they emerged onto the nearby streets, they started a brawl, necessitating the police arresting some of them. It was a disgraceful exhibition of hooliganism, and I remember our children, who were young at the time, being quite scared by it. Let us suppose that some passers-by on the street witnessed this disgusting behaviour. While they might justifiably condemn this behaviour and be repulsed by it, it would be completely irrational of them to reach any of the following conclusions:

- All Mariners supporters are like this.
- This kind of behaviour accurately reflects the ethos and values of the Mariners Football Club.
- The Mariners football team, therefore, does not exist, because no real football club would permit such behaviour amongst its members.

No sensible person would make these kinds of irrational assumptions based upon the poor behaviour of some supporters. Yet, these are exactly the kinds of assumptions that are often made in regard to Christianity, based upon the abhorrent behaviour of some "supporters". The obvious hypocrisy of some so-called Christians leads many people to conclude that;

- Most Christians are hypocrites
- Christianity has no moral merit
- There is no God, because a God who actually exists would never allow such behaviour amongst His followers

The first thing to say in response to all this, is to point out that the merits of any religion must be evaluated on its actual teachings, rather than on the contradictory behaviours of some who profess to be adherents. In the case of Christianity, the teachings of Jesus Christ are utterly opposed to the kinds of appalling behaviour that some who claim to be Christians exhibit. Jesus and the New Testament writers all proclaimed that those who follow God should turn from sin and live wholesome lives that honour God. They spoke of turning from sexual sin, from greed, from hatred and from selfishness. They spoke of living lives that are characterised by *"love, joy, peace, patience, kindness, goodness, faithfulness, gentleness and self-control"* (Galatians 5:22-23). This is the teaching of true Christianity, and it is this kind of teaching that must be evaluated if Christianity is to be fairly assessed.

What can we say, then, about those who call themselves Christians, yet flagrantly flout the teachings of Jesus? We must conclude that there is a very strong possibility that they are not

Christians at all. Jesus made this very point when He said, "*If you love me you will obey my commands*" (John 14:15). A few verses later, in that same passage in John's Gospel, Jesus repeats this important declaration; "*Anyone who loves me will obey my teaching. My Father will love them, and we will come to them and make our home with them. Anyone who does not love me will not obey my teaching*" (John 14:23-24). Later in the New Testament, this message is repeated, "Everyone who loves has been born of God and knows God. Whoever does not love does not know God, because God is love" (1 John 4:7-8). In other words, the true test of whether someone is a Christian, is not what they profess with their lips, but how they live their lives. This is what Jesus was referring to when He said;

"Watch out for false prophets. They come to you in sheep's clothing, but inwardly they are ferocious wolves. By their fruit you will recognize them. Do people pick grapes from thornbushes, or figs from thistles? Likewise, every good tree bears good fruit, but a bad tree bears bad fruit. A good tree cannot bear bad fruit, and a bad tree cannot bear good fruit. Every tree that does not bear good fruit is cut down and thrown into the fire. Thus, by their fruit you will recognize them" (Matthew 7:15-20).

This passage reveals just how abhorrent hypocrisy is to God. Those who claim to know Him but clearly do not, and who bring His Holy Name into disrepute by their unholy lives, will eventually suffer the fire of His wrath. While we might detest hypocrisy, God detests it even more!

There is an important message here for seekers and sceptics who have been turned away from Christianity by hypocrisy. You cannot judge Christianity by the lives of people who aren't really Christians! That would be irrational. In the same way, I cannot judge Indian food by tasting sausages mixed with a teaspoon of curry powder, prepared by someone who has no idea about Indian cooking. To assess something fairly, I must taste the real thing, rather than the poor counterfeit. In the case of Christianity, it must be assessed by investigating the real thing, rather than the fake. And the real thing is found in the life and teachings of Jesus. A person wanting to fairly investigate and assess Christianity should read the accounts of the life of its founder, in the four Gospels of the New Testament; Matthew, Mark, Luke and John. Here you will not only find teaching that is profound and liberating, but you will also encounter the most loving, compassionate, wise person who ever lived.

At this point, the seeker or sceptic might argue, *"If there truly is a God, why does He let hypocrites defame His Name? Why does He let them get away with their terrible behaviour – behaviour that turns people away? Surely, if God exists, He would not let this happen. Therefore, He does not exist!"* There is a philosophical answer to this objection, and a Biblical answer.

The philosophical answer revolves around the complex interplay between God's sovereignty and mankind's free will. Why does God let anyone get away with poor behaviour? It appears that in order to have a meaningful universe, a universe where our decisions have any meaning at all, free will is absolutely essential. A universe where God constantly intervened to over-ride our free wills, to thwart or overturn our actions, would render the very laws of nature unreliable and would negate the essence of such virtues as love and faithfulness. The fact that God allows free will to run its course does not, in any way, prove His non-existence. We have already discussed the very high probability that God, in allowing all kinds of difficult circumstances to unfold in our world, has inscrutable higher purposes at play, purposes that we, mere humans, cannot possibly conceive or understand with our limited perspectives. The same factors that cause God to allow irreligious people to act badly, and temporarily seem to get away with it, also allow self-professed religious people to act badly.

The Biblical answer to the question of why God doesn't intervene to stop so-called Christians behaving badly, centres around a parable that Jesus once told. It is worth quoting in full:

"The kingdom of heaven is like a man who sowed good seed in his field. But while everyone was sleeping, his enemy came and sowed weeds among the wheat, and went away. When the wheat sprouted and formed heads, then the weeds also appeared.

"The owner's servants came to him and said, 'Sir, didn't you sow good seed in your field? Where then did the weeds come from?' "'An enemy did this,' he replied. "The servants asked him, 'Do you want us to go and pull them up?' "'No,' he answered, 'because while you are pulling the weeds, you may uproot some wheat with them. Let both grow together until the harvest. At that time, I will tell the harvesters: First collect the weeds and tie them in bundles to be burned; then gather the wheat and bring it into my barn." (Matthew 13:24-30)

This is an important parable for a number of reasons. Firstly, it corroborates the fact that not everyone who claims to be a Christian is, in fact, a Christian. In God's *"field"* (the church on earth) there are *"weeds"* (people who are not truly Christians) mixed in with the *"wheat"* (those who are genuinely following Christ). Secondly, the parable states unequivocally that these *"weeds"* will one day suffer the fire of God's wrath. In other words, those who claim to be part of God's kingdom but who are not, will one day be on the receiving end of God's extreme displeasure. Finally, it portrays God as withholding His judgment on these *"weeds"* for the present time. His reason for so doing is, no doubt, the same as His reason for withholding judgment on all people, that He might give them ample time to repent in order that some may still be saved; *"The Lord is not slow in keeping his promise, as some understand slowness. Instead he is patient with you, not wanting anyone to perish, but everyone to come to repentance"* (2 Peter 3:9).

The detestable crimes that are sometimes perpetrated by people who claim to be followers of Christ are abhorrent to God and to any true Christian. The vile actions that we see portrayed in the media all too regularly, directly contradict the teachings of Christ and do not reflect true Christianity. Similarly, the perpetrators cannot, under any definition of the term, be said to be Christians, for to be a follower of Christ is to obey Him.

Having said that, an important qualification must be added; all Christians sin. We do not always follow Christ perfectly. We remain fallible until our dying day, regularly requiring Christ's forgiveness. A Christian is not someone who has arrived at a state of perfect obedience. For this reason, Christians can, occasionally, let you down. It is possible for a Christian, in a moment of weakness, to behave poorly, and, in that moment, fail to exemplify the values and morals of Christ's teachings. Using the metaphor of Jesus' parable, as well as God's field (the church) being infested with *"weeds"* (people who are not genuine Christians), some of the wheat plants (genuine Christians) can occasionally, momentarily, manifest *"weed-like"* behaviour. In the case of Christians who are very new to the faith, these "slip-ups" may be frequent and obvious. The difference between the weeds and the wheat, however, is that the true followers of Christ are earnestly seeking to follow and obey Him, despite occasionally slipping up, whereas the *"weeds"* are deliberately, wilfully and habitually living in disobedience to Christ's commands, while outwardly maintaining a religious façade that may be quite convincing. This is why it is extremely difficult to determine who are truly Christ's followers and who are not; to distinguish between the wheat and the weeds. It is also why, in the parable, when the servants offer to pull up all the weeds, the owner of the field tells them not to, *"because while you are pulling the weeds, you may uproot some wheat with them"* (Matt 13:29). Ultimately, only God knows who the true followers of Christ are, and He will weed out those who are not His followers at *"the harvest"* at the end of time (Matt 13:30).

In the meantime, I need to reiterate, in the strongest possible terms, that the poor behaviour of people who profess to be Christians neither disproves God's existence, nor devalues His character. God is a perfect God, worshipped by imperfect creatures. He is in the business of transforming lives, of turning sinners into saints, and this is often a slow and messy process. The seeker who is trying to understand the Christian faith and believe in the God of the Bible, should not be preoccupied with the stumbling steps of Christ's followers or the hypocritical actions of false believers, but, rather, should focus on Christ Himself, who lived a perfect life and whose teaching is truly transformative.

RELIGIOUS VIOLENCE AND WARS

A related issue, that is equally problematic for people who are investigating Christianity, is the issue of religious violence and religiously inspired wars. In this case, we are speaking about the church as a whole behaving badly, rather than just individuals behaving badly. The objection, often articulated by sceptics, goes something like this; *"Christianity is supposed to be about love and peace, but the reality is that it has been the cause of horrific wars throughout history and continues to incite hatred and violence today. If this is what Christianity does, I want nothing to do with it!"* Proponents of this objection cite numerous examples to substantiate their argument, including the Christian Crusades, the Inquisitions, and the killing and fighting between Protestants and Catholics in Northern Ireland. In an editorial in the Sunday Age newspaper, journalist Michael Coulter, wrote about this very issue, concluding, *"The question I can't escape is why so many people prefer the realm of faith, the realm of the Inquisition, to the realm of secular reason."*[1] In other words, how can people follow Christianity, when it has been responsible for so much killing?

What can be said in response to this? Firstly, let us analyse each of these supposed incidents of Christian violence.

THE CRUSADES

The Crusades are often portrayed as a Christian offensive, mounted against the peace-loving Muslims of the Middle East. But nothing could be further from the truth! The Crusades were a belated counter-offensive to liberate large areas of the Middle East that had been conquered and subjugated by the invading Muslim army. Joe Carter, in his article, *"The Truth About The Crusades"*, explains;

"In the year 600, most of the Middle East, from present-day Turkey to Iraq, including Egypt and the southern Mediterranean

coast, was Christian, and its principal cities— including Alexandria, Antioch, Damascus and Jerusalem—were vibrant centres of Christian life and culture. Within a century the entire region came under Muslim rule."[2]

From 622 to 750 A.D. the Muslim army swept across the Middle East, capturing city after city, killing an estimated 60 million innocent people and subjugating the survivors. Property and houses were seized, and the original occupants were dispossessed. For the next three hundred years the original inhabitants cried out for justice, asking the Western world to liberate them from their invaders and restore their lands and their homes to them. Finally, and very belatedly, the Western nations, under the instigation of the Kings of England and France, mounted a campaign to liberate these conquered territories from their oppressors. This campaign was blessed by the Pope, and declared to be a righteous war in response to unjust tyranny and oppression. The Crusades were conducted over a period of 300 years, in a series of campaigns, commencing in the 11th century. An estimated six million people died during these battles, and the crusades were only partially effective in liberating some cities.

An important question has to be asked at this point: Why are the Crusades referred to as a religious war when, in almost every aspect, this campaign was identical to the Second World War? World War II was sparked by a hostile aggressor, Germany, invading a peaceful nation, Poland. Poland cried out for justice, and the Western world banded together to mount a counter-offensive to liberate Poland and to stem the tide of Germany's ongoing invasion of Europe. Similar to the Crusades, the Western counter-offensive had the blessing of the Christian church, which prayed for God's strength for the

Allied forces as they sought to liberate Europe from the oppressive invasion of the German army. There is no significant difference between the Crusades and the Allied campaign in World War II. Both campaigns were counter-offensives to liberate an oppressed people, and both were blessed by the Christian church. The Crusades were no more Christian than was the World War II counter-offensive; the Western armies of both campaigns contained a mixture of Christians and non-Christians, and can only be described as "Christian" in the sense that the countries represented were "Christian" nations. Yet World War II is popularly viewed as a righteous, secular war, whereas the Crusades are often condemned as a religious war, with Christians being portrayed as the invaders! This is a severe misconstruction of history, which seems to have been enshrined as unassailable truth. Joe Carter comments on this, and laments how difficult it is to reverse this popular impression;

"So deep is this paradigm—the Crusades as Western Christian aggression, not a defensive movement of Christian piety—that the writings of mere historians can do little to undo the damage. Jonathan Riley Smith, a distinguished historian of the Crusades, once said that he had given up hope that scholarly writing could make a difference."[3]

Many sceptics point to the atrocities committed by some supposedly "Christian" Crusaders as a further indictment of Christianity; Muslim soldiers were tortured, towns were plundered, and Muslim women were raped. We are right to condemn these heinous actions as war crimes. Yet two points must be made in response.

Firstly, we must reiterate that the Crusaders were a Western army not a Christian army. As was the case with the allied forces in World War II, the vast majority of soldiers in the Crusader army were non-Christians. They were Christian in name only – having been recruited from "Christian" nations. In fact, at the time of the Crusades, the Western world was barely emerging from the Dark Ages, which was characterised by widespread ignorance of the true gospel of Christ. Syncretistic religious superstition abounded, and those who had properly understood the message of Christ and had responded to Him in faith and repentance were in the extreme minority. It is difficult to conceive of genuine Christians, who love Christ and are seeking to live in obedience to His morals and commands, raping and torturing people.

Secondly, the sad fact is that war crimes of this kind have been committed in almost every war in human history, including the two World Wars, Vietnam, Afghanistan and Iraq. War seems to attract not only decent men and women with a desire to be agents of justice and to defend the defenceless, but also a minority of unbalanced individuals with a blood-lust for murder and violence. These individuals who "go off the reservation" and commit war crimes deserve to be prosecuted, but their detestable actions do not invalidate the righteous necessity (or otherwise) of the various campaigns.

The accusation that the Crusades represent the violent aggression of Christianity is completely unsubstantiated by a proper reading of the facts of history.

THE INQUISITIONS

The Inquisitions were a series of ecclesiastical (church) tribunals, established by Popes and bishops, over an extended period of time, from the 12th century until the early 19th

century. The primary aim of the Inquisitions was to deal with heresy by bringing to trial all those within the church who promoted doctrines contradicting the official teachings of the Roman Catholic Church. Those who refused to recant their supposedly heretical teachings were incarcerated or, on some occasions, executed by burning at the stake. The most famous, and violent, Inquisition was the Spanish Inquisition (1478 – 1834), but this was merely one of many. Inquisitions took place predominantly in France, Italy and Spain, and there were no Inquisitions in England or North Eastern Europe.

Many sceptics point to the religious Inquisitions of the Middle Ages as examples of intolerance and violence perpetrated by Christianity. I have heard sceptics claim that hundreds of thousands, or even millions, of people were sentenced to death by these Inquisitions, and these "facts" are used as arguments to reject Christianity. What are we to make of these claims and how are we to respond?

Firstly, it is important to correct the gross exaggeration that has taken place regarding the Inquisitions. Claims, by opponents of the Church, of huge numbers of deaths at the hands of the Inquisitors, have, in recent years, been overturned by contemporary historical scholarship, prompted by the release, in recent decades, of official Vatican records of the Inquisitions. Research by Dr. Edward Peters[4] and Prof. Henry Kamen[5] are at the forefront of an emerging new perspective on the Inquisitions. Their research, and that of others, indicates that a much smaller number of people were sentenced to death by the Inquisitions than was previously thought. For example, Dr. Kamen states,

"Taking into account all the tribunals of Spain up until

about 1530, it is unlikely that more than two thousand people were executed for heresy by the Inquisition."[6]

Furthermore, Dr. Peters, in assessing the death toll in the ensuing period of history, writes,

"The best estimate is that around 3000 death sentences were carried out in Spain by Inquisitorial verdict between 1550 and 1800, a far smaller number than in comparable secular courts."[7]

Of course, this does not excuse or justify these death sentences, but merely provides us with a factual basis upon which to comment. If we are going to discuss Inquisitional deaths, let us at least get the facts right!

This more accurate assessment of the death toll, however, is still damning. How can the execution of thousands of people, simply for their divergent beliefs, be reconciled to a religion of love and peace? The simple answer is, it can't! At this point I need to make an extremely important, and controversial, distinction. The religious Inquisitions were not conducted by Christians. They were sanctioned and conducted by the institutional Roman Catholic Church which, in the Middle Ages, was a very long way from being genuinely Christian.

The period from 500 A.D. to 1500 A.D. are known as the Dark Ages of the Church. During this period the true understanding of the Gospel of Christ was largely lost within the institutional Church. There were no denominations; the one Church on earth was the Roman Catholic Church, and its official teaching flowed directly from the Pope and his Cardinals. The Bible was only translated into Latin and all other translations were outlawed. Because most priests could not read Latin, (as it was a very academic language), very few priests had ever read the Bible, and were largely ignorant of its teachings. Furthermore, because priestly appointments could be quite lucrative, the priesthood became a popular profession, attracting many people who were unconverted. Consequently, sexual immorality amongst the clergy was rampant. In major cities and towns there were high class brothels that were dedicated to servicing the priests. Many priests also set up a woman in lodgings in his town or village, and kept her as his unofficial wife. This practice was well-known and silently accepted by the priest's local parishioners, who turned a blind eye to the practice. Even many of the Popes were well-known for having numerous mistresses. For example, Wikipedia lists six Popes who fathered illegitimate children, a further eight Popes who had affairs without fathering children, and four Popes who had homosexual affairs.[8] Furthermore, priests who had ambition, could purchase a better parish for themselves, by paying the Vatican large sums of money. Similarly, priests often ascended the ecclesiastical hierarchy, becoming Bishops and Cardinals, by purchasing these positions from the Vatican.

The official teachings of the Roman Catholic Church during the Middles Ages became polluted with all kinds of medieval superstition. Supposed relics of dead saints were said to have magical powers, and the church charged people money to touch them. Greed and corruption added further to the polluting of Christian doctrine. Forgiveness of sins was sold for money. People could buy an "Indulgence", and official certificate signed by a bishop or, on special occasions, by the Pope himself, absolving them of their sins. The church also introduced the concept of purgatory, and consequently sold more Indulgences, which supposedly enabled people to pay money to free their dead relatives from the flames of torment. One famous priest who was particularly effective in selling these indulgences on behalf of the Pope and various bishops, was

Johann Tetzel (1465-1519), who coined the catch-cry, *"When a coin in the coffers rings, a soul from purgatory springs"*[9]. The sale of these Indulgences, as well as charges for access to relics, brought huge amounts of money into the coffers of the Roman Catholic Church. Sadly, it also completely undermined the Gospel of grace. People were taught to trust in purchased certificates for their forgiveness, rather than in Christ. Both priests and laity alike knew no better, for very few people could read Latin and, therefore, had no access to the teachings of the Bible. Those few individuals who did gain an understanding of the teachings of Christ, and who dared to voice beliefs that differed from the official dogma of the Church, were, themselves, brought before the Inquisition, and charged with heresy.

It was truly a grim, dark period in the Church's history. The institutional Roman Catholic Church was corrupt, superstitious, immoral and controlling. The true Gospel was largely lost, and genuine Christianity among laity and clergy was a rare thing.

The Inquisitions, therefore, must be seen in this context. They do not represent the actions of the genuine Christian Church, but of a religious institution that had drifted a long way from true Christianity. Significantly, when Martin Luther and others emerged in the 16th century and led a movement that sought to re-institute Biblical Christianity, including the publishing of Bibles in the common language, the Roman Catholic Church condemned them as heretics and put some of them to death. This highlights the fact that the Roman Catholic Inquisitions were not Christian, and arose from a religious institution that directly opposed genuine, Biblical Christianity.

Christians today look back with horror and disgust at the Inquisitions, seeing them for what they truly are; one more appalling example of false religion. Many of the practices and teachings of the Roman Catholic Church during the Middle Ages, including the Inquisitions, are in direct conflict with the teachings of Christ, and cannot be said to reflect true Christianity. If Christianity is to be assessed fairly, it must be assessed on the basis of the teachings of Christ and the Bible, rather than the false teachings and practices of the Dark Ages.

THE NORTHERN IRELAND "TROUBLES"

The 30-year conflict between Catholics and Protestants in Northern Ireland, commencing on 5 October 1968 and ending on 10 April 1998, is often cited as another ugly example of Christian hatred and violence. During this conflict, an estimated 3,000 people were killed, and a further 50,000 people were injured.

An important point of clarification, however, must be made. This conflict does not represent two groups of Christians fighting each other. It was a political and territorial conflict that split the entire nation into two violently opposed positions. An article on the official BBC website confirms the nature of the conflict; *"This was a territorial conflict, not a religious one"*[10]. The larger percentage of Northern Ireland's population wished to remain part of the United Kingdom, and they identified themselves as predominantly Protestants, while the minority of the population who wished to become part of the Republic of Ireland, identified as predominantly Catholic. In the case of the vast majority of the population, however, their identification as either Protestant or Catholic, was political rather than religious. An individual's identification as with one group or the other did not, and still does not, infer that they ever attend a church service, or even that they believe in God. Similarly, in Australia, when the National Census occurs every 5 years, there are millions of people who tick "Catholic" or "Anglican", who never darken the door of a church from one year to the next. This kind of casual religious affiliation tends to be more a reflection of historic allegiance, rather than an expression of personal, active faith. The stated religious affiliations within Northern Ireland are of exactly the same nature, and the violence between the two groups has no relevance to a discussion of genuine Christianity.

SECULAR VIOLENCE

Earlier this chapter, I quoted Michael Coulter, a journalist for the Sunday Age newspaper, who wrote; *"The question I can't escape is why so many people prefer the realm of faith, the realm of the Inquisition, to the realm of secular reason."*[11] Having debunked the false idea that the Inquisitions represented genuine Christianity, it is worth commenting on Coulter's expressed preference for *"the realm of secular reason"*. Surely Coulter has not considered the extremely poor humanitarian track record of secular philosophy, for secular regimes have been responsible for the deaths of millions of innocent people. The following list provides rough estimates of the unthinkable number of deaths caused by secular regimes:

DEATHS PERPETRATED BY SECULAR REGIMES	
Nazi killing of Jews	6,000,000
Nazi killing of gypsies and minority ethnic groups	9,000,000
Stalin's purges	60,000,000
Communist China's purges	72,000,000
Cambodian genocide (under Pol Pot)	2,000,000
Ugandan genocide	200,000
Rwandan genocide	500,000
TOTAL:	149,700,000[106]

Nearly 150 million people killed, and that is only the death toll from secular regimes over the last 100 years! There would be countless millions who have suffered similar fates at the hands of cruel secular regimes of the past. If sceptics are dismissing Christianity because of its supposedly violent track record (which I strongly dispute!), how can they possibly justify placing their faith in secular philosophy?

GOD-ORDAINED KILLING IN THE OLD TESTAMENT

We cannot leave this topic without discussing the issue of God-ordained killing in the Old Testament. This falls under two categories; capital punishment for specific sins, and God's instruction to the Israelites to destroy neighbouring nations. Both of these are problematic for many people who are seeking to believe in the God of the Bible.

Capital Punishment In The Old Testament

The Old Testament prescribed the death penalty for a number of crimes:

- Murder (Exodus 21:12-14; Leviticus 24:17,21)
- Attacking or cursing a parent (Exodus 21:15,17)
- Disobedience to parents (Deuteronomy 21:18-21)
- Kidnapping (Exodus 21:16)
- Failure to confine a dangerous animal, resulting in death (Exodus 21:28-29)
- Witchcraft and sorcery (Exodus 22:18, Leviticus 20:27, Deuteronomy 13:5, 1 Samuel 28:9)
- Human sacrifice (Leviticus 20:2-5)
- Sex with an animal (Exodus 22:19, Leviticus 20:16)
- Incest (Leviticus 18:6-18, 20:11-12,14,17,19-21)
- Adultery (Leviticus 20:10; Deuteronomy 22:22)
- Homosexual acts (Leviticus 20:13)
- Prostitution by a priest's daughter (Leviticus 21:9)
- Blasphemy (Leviticus 24:14,16, 23)
- False prophecy (Deuteronomy 18:20)
- Perjury in capital cases (Deuteronomy 19:16-19)
- Refusing to obey a decision of a judge or priest (Deuteronomy 17:12)
- False claim of a woman's virginity at time of marriage (Deuteronomy 22:13-21)
- Sex between a woman pledged to be married and a man other than her betrothed (Deuteronomy 22:23-24)

These death penalties represent a stage of God's progressive revelation, as He dealt with an infant nation and sought to establish and reinforce strong rules that would preserve the moral and religious integrity of His people. Weaker punishments would not have been effective as a deterrent, and would have led to many more people succumbing to sin and falling away. As harsh as these punishments seem to us today, they ensured that by the time the Messiah was born, there was a remnant of Israel who were still faithful to God, some of whom would be ready to follow the Saviour. There are 83 nations in the world today that still have capital punishment, 54 of which have implemented capital punishment within the last decade[12]. The fact that a nation, or religion, may uphold capital punishment as part of their judicial system is not cause, in itself, to condemn that nation or religion. The objection, by sceptics, to the Old Testament's death penalties, arises, not so much from a philosophical objection to capital punishment, but from their disagreement with the morals being reinforced. And that is another topic!

God's Instructions To The Israelites To Attack Other Nations

It is undeniable that God ordered the killing of various groups of people in the Old Testament. The most significant example of God-ordained killing is His instructions to the Jewish nation, as they entered the promised land of Canaan. These instructions varied from city to city. In some instances, God's instruction was that the Jews should *"drive the inhabitants from the land"* (Num 33:55). At other times God specifically ordered that the inhabitants of a city be *"destroyed"* (Deut 20:17). What are we to make of this? Dr. Andrew Shead, professor of Old Testament at Moore Theological College, Sydney, writes;

> "The Mosaic accounts indicate that total annihilation of the Canaanites was not what God directed, but total destruction of them in terms of military victory, resulting in their complete eviction from the land. This is inferred from passages that subsequently warn the Israelites not to adopt their religious practices or intermarry with them (Josh 23:12-13). Verbs of expulsion are more commonly used than verbs of killing to describe the conquest (Lev 18:24-28; Num 33:51-56; 2 Kings 16:3). Many Canaanites were neither killed nor expelled (2 Sam 24:7; 1 Kings 9:15-23). Additionally, Mosaic ethics outline more humane treatment for non-combatant enemies (Exod 22:24)."[13]

Furthermore, it is important that we understand that God was not driving the former inhabitants out, or killing them, simply because they were an inconvenience for the Jews who wished to inhabit the land. The Canaanites had come under God's judgment for their many atrocities, including centuries of human sacrifice (usually of children), witchcraft, immorality, torture, genocide and idolatry. Ancient literature indicates the depth of the depravity of the Canaanites and surrounding nations at that time.[14] Hence, we read God's pronouncement in Deuteronomy 9:4-6, "*It is on account of the wickedness of these nations that the Lord is going to drive them out*". God had been warning these nations for decades or even centuries, through various prophets, to turn from their sins (Genesis 15, Genesis 18, Joshua 2).

It is worth noting that, in Deuteronomy, there are THREE TIMES as many instructions to drive the inhabitants out of the land as there are to kill or destroy them. So, it seems that even in the execution of God's judgment upon these people, there were degrees of sin that required degrees of punishment. The sins of some cities and nations were so horrendous that they had forfeited the right to live, while others were simply dispossessed and given further time to repent of their sins.

Even as God was executing His justice upon these nations, if anyone repented and submitted to Him, God relented and forgave them. Rahab and her family are a case in point. This illustrates the principle that *"God does not require the death of a sinner, but that all should turn to Him and live"* (Ezek 18:23).

In the case of those who were killed under God's instruction, we need to view this in the light of eternity. Our brief mortal lives are the merest, fleeting shadow compared to the infinitude of eternity that is to come. God was merely bringing forward their eternal punishment by a few years or decades; cutting short their lives and taking them straight to judgment. In doing so, God, in His infinite, all-seeing wisdom, may well have determined that these people would never have repented and, furthermore, may have led many others astray if they had been left alive. In many ways, we sophisticated 21st century citizens place too much value upon this brief mortal existence, and not nearly enough value upon the eternal existence that lies beyond the doorway of death.

One has to consider whether a certain point is reached where the evil perpetrated by some people is so serious that they have forfeited the right to live. The Old Testament indicates that, in God's eyes, capital punishment was warranted, not just for some individuals, but for whole cities. Those of us with a moral conscience want God to be a God of justice who does not allow evil to go unpunished. If this is what we demand of a just God, it is illogical to ask, *"Why doesn't God do anything about all the evil in the world?"*, and then criticise God when He **does** do something about it!

Yet despite their wickedness, Canaanites who turned in repentance to follow the God of Israel were forgiven and enfolded into Israel (eg, Rahab and her family, Joshua 6:25). At no point in the Bible were the Israelites directed by God to kill anyone simply because they did not worship Yahweh. In fact, the Scriptures indicate that God is patient, not desiring the death of a sinner, but that all should turn to him in repentance (Ezek 33:11). This is very different from the teaching of some other religions, which teach that those who refuse to convert should be killed, and who view such killing as blessed by their god.

Reflection Questions

1. What new insights have you gained from this chapter? Has this chapter changed any of your views?

2. What questions or challenges has this chapter raised for you?

3. Read John 14:15-24. What is the relationship between these exhortations to "obey" and the doctrine of grace? What implications does this passage have for use as we seek to be witnesses for Christ?

4. Read 1 Peter 2:11-12. What implications does this have for our consideration of the issue of Christians behaving badly?

5. Read Matthew 13:24-30. What does this reveal about the nature of the church? How does it explain God's apparent lack of action in not dealing severely with wayward or fake Christians?

6. Read Matthew 7:15-20. How does this reinforce the

concepts that are present in the Parable of the Weeds? Are there any new elements?

7. How can we help people who have been turned off Christianity by Christians behaving badly?

8. Have <u>you</u> been wounded by Christians behaving badly? How have you dealt with this?

9. Read Ephesians 5:25-27. This compares Christ's love for His church to a husband's love for his beautiful bride. How can this help us to deal with disappointments with the church? How should this influence our own attitude to Christ's church?

TWELVE

GOD AND EVOLUTION

The theory of evolution is a major stumbling block for many people in seeking to believe in the God of the Bible. The popular impression is that the theory of evolution is supported by a vast body of evidence, and that the theory, in itself, disproves the existence of God. Neither of these propositions are accurate.

THE THEORY OF EVOLUTION DOES NOT DISPROVE THE EXISTENCE OF GOD

There are Christians, both scientists and non-scientists, who believe that God used the process of evolution to create life. They see no conflict between their Christian faith, and the process of evolution. I am not of this opinion, but there are plenty of intelligent people who hold this position. This view is commonly referred to as "theistic evolution". A survey of American churches in 2007 revealed that 51% of Protestants and 58% of Catholics believe that God used evolution to create life[1]. Amongst the scientific community, there are scientists at the cutting edge of their fields who have published academic papers and books reconciling their Christian faith with their belief in evolution. For example, Dr. Francis Collins, a respected geneticist and the head of the Human Genome Project, published a book, *"The Language of God; A Scientist Presents Evidence For Belief"*[2], in which he argued that the evolutionary process is completely consistent with the God of the Bible.

The reason why some Christians have no problem believing in the theory of evolution is that it is not essentially a theory about origins, but about *processes*. It proposes a possible explanation about the processes by which the variety of species that we see today may have developed. But it has nothing to say about the origin of the universe itself. The theory of evolution assumes that the earth, and the whole universe, was already existent when organic life began, and it proposes no explanation for its existence. Furthermore, the theory has no scientifically satisfactory explanation as to how a lifeless, inorganic universe could have produced living, organic matter in the first instance. For the answers to these key questions, Christians turn to the Bible and to their faith in a transcendent Creator God.

In fact, people who believe in evolution who do **not** have a belief in a Creator are left with a huge problem; how to explain the origin of the universe itself. Until recent decades, atheists have maintained that the universe has always existed. This belief in the eternal existence of the universe was upheld from the time of Aristotle (350 B.C.) until the mid-20th century, and it effectively removed the necessity to believe in a Creator. Outspoken atheist, Bertrand Russell (1872 - 1970) once famously stated, *"The universe is just there and that's all."* However, several very significant scientific discoveries in the latter half of the 20th century have completely overturned this view. These discoveries include:

- 1915: Extrapolations from Einstein's Theory of Relativity, which predicted, from a purely theoretical point of view, that the universe, including time itself, had a beginning. These extrapolations were deeply disconcerting to atheists.
- 1927: Alexander Friedmann and Georges Lemaitre (astronomer and Belgian priest), extrapolated Einstein's theories further, and predicting that, if Einstein's theories are correct, the universe must be expanding and, as a corollary, must have originated from a single point in the distant past.
- 1929: Edwin Hubble provided the first visual confirmation of the expansion of the universe. From an observatory at Mount Wilson, USA, he observed and measured the doppler red-shift effect of light emanating from observable galaxies. This was the first physical evidence that confirmed what had only been a theory until this point. Hubble also concurred with the conclusions of Friedman and

Lemaitre that the universe, including time itself, must have originated from a single initial point in the space-time continuum.

- 1964: Drs Arno Penzias and Robert Wilson discovered and measured Cosmic Microwave Background Radiation that exists in the space between galaxies; radiation with a frequency and ambient temperature that cannot be accounted for by the surrounding galaxies. The only logical explanation is that it is vestigial – an echo of cataclysmic events from the beginning of the universe itself. They won a Nobel Prize for this ground-breaking discovery.

As a result of these and other advances in the science of cosmology, the once-convenient belief in the eternal existence of the universe has now been completely repudiated. Even renowned atheist, Stephen Hawking, was forced to concede this shocking development, stating;

"All the evidence seems to indicate, that the universe has not existed forever, but that it had a beginning. This is probably the most remarkable discovery of modern cosmology."[3]

Stephen Hawking continues;

"We have made tremendous progress in cosmology in the last hundred years. The General Theory of Relativity and the discovery of the expansion of the universe has shattered the old picture of an ever-existing and ever-lasting universe. The discovery of Cosmic Microwave Background Radiation also supports this conclusion. This is a profound change in our picture of the universe and of reality itself."[4]

Hawking is correct; it *is* a profound change in the way we

view the universe. Because if the universe had a beginning, it begs the question: Who put it there? How can **nothing** become **something** unless **someone** beyond the universe creates it? The cosmological evidence for the universe having a beginning cries out for a supernatural explanation, because only something **outside** of nature ("supernatural") can possibly create nature. Nature cannot create itself out of nothing!

Dr Robert Jastrow, astronomer, physicist and founder of NASA's Goddard Institute of Space Studies, states,

"Astronomers now find they have painted themselves into a corner because they have proven, by their own methods, that the world began abruptly in an act of creation to which you can trace the seeds of every star, every planet, every living thing in this cosmos and on the earth. And they have found that all this happened as a product of forces they cannot hope to discover. That there are what I or anyone would call supernatural forces at work is now, I think, a scientifically proven fact."[5]

Similarly, Dr James Clerk Maxwell, physicist and mathematician, who is credited with formulating classical electromagnetic theory and whose contributions to science are considered to be of the same magnitude to those of Einstein and Newton, stated,

"Science is incompetent to reason upon the creation of matter itself out of nothing. We have reached the utmost limit of our thinking faculties when we have admitted that because matter cannot be eternal and self-existent it must have been created."[6]

Commenting on the growing number of scientists who now concede that the universe must have a supernatural cause, astrophysicist, Dr Hugh Ross, Director of Observations at Royal Astronomical Society, Vancouver, states;

"Astronomers who do not draw theistic or deistic conclusions are becoming rare, and even the few dissenters hint that the tide is against them. Geoffrey Burbidge, of the University of California at San Diego, complains that his fellow astronomers are rushing off to join 'the First Church of Christ of the Big Bang.'"[7]

Dr Hugh Ross continues;

"All the data accumulated in the twentieth and twenty-first centuries tell us that a transcendent Creator must exist. For all the matter, energy, nine space dimensions, and even time, each suddenly and simultaneously came into being from some source beyond itself. Likewise, it is valid to refer to the Creator as transcendent, for the act of causing these effects must take place outside or independent of them."[8]

So, the first important point to make in our discussion of God and evolution, is that the theory of evolution does not even come ***close*** to disproving the existence of God. In fact, it has absolutely nothing to say about the most important question of all: Where did the universe come from in the beginning? And, as I am about to demonstrate, at the same time as the scientific community is turning towards a supernatural explanation for the origin of the universe, the evidence base for the theory of evolution, as a description of the process of species development, is rapidly diminishing.

THE THEORY OF EVOLUTION HAS A DIMINISHING EVIDENCE BASE

I have written extensively on this topic, on my website, www.SmartFaith.net, where you can find significantly more information than I can fit into a single chapter of a book. However, here is a brief overview of the growing case against evolution.

In popular media the impression is given that the theory of evolution has been unequivocally proven. Not only is this not the case, but scientific developments in recent decades have seriously undermined much of the evidence previously used to support the theory. The reality is that the theory of evolution is in serious trouble today, and there are a growing number of respected scientists who are abandoning the theory in favour of a more theistic explanation for the origin of the universe. The average person on the street would not be aware of this trend, because the significant problems in the theory are not being discussed in popular media. At academic levels, however, the serious flaws in the theory are beginning to emerge.

In recent years, a number of academic papers and books have been published, discussing these flaws. One such work is *"More than Myth"* (Chartwell Press, 2014, Editors: Robert Stackpole and Paul Brown). Of particular significance is the chapter, *"Top 10 Scientific Problems With Biological and Chemical Evolution"* by Dr. Casey Luskin. Below is a brief summary of the 10 problems suggested by Luskin (in his own words):

1. Lack of a viable mechanism for producing high levels of complex and specified genetic information. Related to this are problems with the Darwinian mechanism producing irreducibly complex features, and the problems of non-functional or deleterious intermediate stages.[9]

2. The failure of the fossil record to provide support for Darwinian evolution.[10]

3. The failure of molecular biology to provide evidence for a grand "tree of life."[11]

4. Natural selection is an extremely inefficient method of spreading traits in populations unless a trait has an extremely high selection coefficient.

5. The problem that convergent evolution appears rampant — at both the genetic and morphological levels, even though under Darwinian theory this is highly unlikely.[12]

6. The failure of chemistry to explain the origin of the genetic code.[13]

7. The failure of developmental biology to explain why vertebrate embryos diverge from the beginning of development.[14]

8. The failure of neo-Darwinian evolution to explain the biogeographical distribution of many species.[15]

9. A long history of inaccurate predictions inspired by Neo-Darwinism regarding vestigial organs or so-called "junk" DNA.[16]

10. Humans show many behavioural and cognitive traits and abilities that offer no apparent survival advantage (e.g. music, art, religion, ability to ponder the nature of the universe).

These are just a few of the many significant problems now facing the theory of evolution. Similarly, in his recent book, "*Evolution Impossible*"[17], Dr John F Ashton suggests twelve reasons why evolution can't explain the origin of life on earth. Some of those reasons are:

1. The Impossibility of a living cell arising by chance

2. Random mutations cannot produce new type of organisms

3. The failure of the evolutionary fossil record

4. The complete absence of evolutionary intermediaries
5. Geological evidence for a catastrophic global flood
6. Historic evidence for a worldwide flood
7. Erosion rates, sedimentation rates and other evidence for a young earth
8. Problems with radiometric dating

These and other significant problems are leading a growing number of the world's leading scientists to either abandon or seriously question the theory of evolution. The book, *"In Six Days"*, edited by Dr John F Ashton[18], has 50 chapters, each written by a different scientist from various parts of the world. Each of them provides extensive scientific arguments for their view that the theory of evolution is no longer scientifically tenable, and they explain the growing scientific evidence supporting theistic creation. The contributing scientists are highly regarded internationally, and come from a wide range of fields including biology, chemistry, biochemistry, genetics, physics, zoology, astronomy, meteorology, engineering and botany.

A large number of non-Christian scientists are now embracing the concept of "intelligent design" as the most likely explanation for the existence of our universe. This is primarily the result growing scientific understanding of the fine tuning of the universal constants which govern our universe, and which are mutually essential for life to exist.

Table of Universal Constants (again!)

Quantity	Symbol	Numerical value	Unit
Acceleration of free fall (standard)	g_n	9.8066	m/s^2
Atmospheric pressure (standard)	p_0	1.0132×10^5	Pa
Atomic mass unit	u	1.6606×10^{-27}	kg
Avogadro constant	N_A	6.0220×10^{23}	mol^{-1}
Bohr magneton	μ_B	9.2741×10^{-24}	J/T, $A\,m^2$
Boltzmann constant	k	1.3807×10^{-23}	J/K
Electron			
charge	$-e$	1.6022×10^{-19}	C
mass	m_e	9.1095×10^{-31}	kg
charge/mass ratio	e/m_e	1.7588×10^{11}	C/kg
Faraday constant	F	9.6485×10^4	C/mol
Free space			
electric constant	ε_0	8.8542×10^{-12}	F/m
intrinsic impedance	Z_0	376.7	Ω
magnetic constant	μ_0	$4\pi \times 10^{-7}$	H/m
speed of electromagnetic waves	c	2.9979×10^8	m/s
Gravitational constant	G	6.6732×10^{-11}	$N\,m^2/kg^2$
Ideal molar gas constant	R	8.3144	$J/(mol\,K)$
Molar volume at s.t.p.	V_m	2.2414×10^{-2}	m^3/mol
Neutron rest mass	m_n	1.6748×10^{-27}	kg
Planck constant	h	6.6262×10^{-34}	J s
normalised	$h/2\pi$	1.0546×10^{-34}	J s
Proton			
charge	$+e$	1.6022×10^{-19}	C
rest mass	m_p	1.6726×10^{-27}	kg
charge/mass ratio	e/m_p	0.9579×10^8	C/kg
Radiation constants	c_1	3.7418×10^{-16}	$W\,m^2$
	c_2	1.4388×10^{-2}	m K
Rydberg constant	R_H	1.0968×10^7	m^{-1}
Stefan-Boltzmann constant	σ_s	5.6703×10^{-8}	$J/(m^2 K^4)$
Wien constant	k_w	2.8978×10^{-3}	m K

The possibility of these universal constants all arriving at their precise values by sheer chance alone is so infinitesimally small as to be an impossibility. The 34 recognised universal constants are so finely tuned that altering one by even one thousandth of one percent would render life and, in the case of some of the constants, the existence of matter itself, impossible. Dr. Robin Collins, Professor of Theoretical Physics, North Western University, states,

"The chance of just two of these cosmological constants developing by sheer chance, is one in 100 million trillion trillion trillion trillion trillion trillion. That's more than the number of atoms in the universe! And that's just TWO of the constants!" [19]

Dr Paul Davies, Professor of Theoretical Physics, Adelaide University, states,

"The physical universe is put together with an ingenuity that is so astonishing, with physical constants that are so impos-

sibly perfect, that I can no longer accept it as the product of brute chance".[20]

Dr. Fred Hoyle, astrophysicist and mathematician, Cambridge University, states,

"*A common sense interpretation of the facts suggests that a super-intellect has monkeyed with physics, as well as with chemistry and biology, and that there are no blind forces worth speaking about in nature. The numbers one calculates from the facts seem to me so overwhelming as to put this conclusion almost beyond question.*"[21]

THE FAILURE OF THE EVOLUTIONARY FOSSIL RECORD

Dr. Roberto Fondi, Professor of Palaeontology at the University of Seaella, Italy comments;

"*The fundamental assumptions upon which evolution is based are not at all confirmed by palaeontology. All the biological groups, from bacteria to humans, appear abruptly in the fossil record, without any links connecting them. If evolution had really happened, the evidence would be in abundance and incontestable. The museums would be overflowing with exhibits clearly documenting the transitions between various biological groups. But the fact is that after nearly two centuries of intense research, there are NO such exhibits. The very few fossils once claimed to be some kind of evolutionary link, such as the amphibians, Ictheostica and Simorea, the bird Archaeopteryx, and the Australopithecine ape, Homohabilis, are, at best, highly questionable.*"[22]

Regarding Archaeopteryx, which was, for decades, one of

the most heralded supposed "missing links", the Encyclopedia Of Evolution, by Dr. Stanley A. Rice, now states;

"Modern birds are not the descendants of Archaeopteryx, which has proved to be an evolutionary dead end. Birds diversified well before Archaeopteryx."[23]

Similarly, the Berkeley University website states, "It has long been accepted that Archaeopteryx was a transitional form between birds and reptiles. However, its feathers, wings, furcula ("wishbone") and reduced fingers are all now acknowledged as being characteristics of some modern birds."[24]

In terms of so-called human evolution, the original missing links, taught up until the 1970's, have now all been disproved; homohabilis, hesperopithecus, Java Man, Piltdown Man, Peking Man, Neanderthal Man and, more lately, Lucy (Australopithecus). These have all proven to be either hoaxes by fanatical atheists or false hopes. For example:

- **Hesperopithecus** was believed to be one such missing link, but in the late 1960's, Henry Fairfield Osborn's field expedition proved beyond doubt that Hesperopithecus was the remains of a modern-day wild pig![25]
- **Java Man** was discovered in 1891 by Eugene Dubois. Yet Dubois also discovered fully human skulls at the same level as Java Man, and concealed them for 30 years. Before he died he confessed this and admitted that Java Man was really a gibbon. Furthermore, Frau Selenka's expedition, in 1907, discovered that the Java Man site was a volcanic area and could not be more than 5000 years old![26]
- **Piltdown Man**, discovered in 1912 by Charles

Dawson, was chemically analysed in 1953 by Prof. Kenneth Oakley, who proved conclusively that the skull was that of a modern human and the jawbone was that of an ape. The bones had been chemically treated by Dawson to make them appear old, and the teeth had been filed down to resemble human teeth. Charles Dawson was disgraced by the eventual unveiling of this fraud, which had fooled the scientific world for 40 years.[27]

- **Neanderthal Man**, discovered in 1848 at Forbes Quarry, Gibraltar, was declared by evolutionists at the time to be THE missing link. In 1939, it was proved by Prof. Sergio Sergi that Neanderthal Man had walked erect, and not on all fours as evolutionists had previously believed. Then, in 1947, a Neanderthal Man was discovered to have lived in a cave AFTER modern man had inhabited it. Neanderthal Man is now known to have been a modern homosapien.[28]

- **Australopithecus Ramidus** was hailed in 1994 to be the latest supposed missing link. Scientists have now unearthed a nearly completed skeleton of the same creature and have had to re-classify it as Ardipithecus Ramidus - a monkey.[29]

- **"Lucy"** (an Australopithecine) is the latest supposed missing link hailed by evolutionists. However, living specimens of this creature have reportedly been discovered in the jungles of Sumatra. The creature, known as Orang Pendek, is simply another variety of the Orang monkey species, and not, as we were told, an ancient ancestor of homo sapiens. The well-known French science journal, "Science et Vie", admitted this fact in its February 1999 issue with the headline "Farewell Lucy" (Adieu Lucy) and the statement that Australopithecus could not be considered the ancestor of man.

THERE ARE NO UNCONTESTED TRANSITIONAL FORMS

The result, in recent years, of more rigorous examination of archaeological evidence, has been the repudiation of all previously held transitional forms. There remains today not one single, uncontested transitional form as evidence for evolution between species.

The Smithsonian Museum in Washington DC is the premier museum in America, and is colloquially considered to be the "head office" of evolution. It used to have an exhibit called *"Origin Of Life: Apes to Man"*, which featured impressive representations of the various transitional ape-man forms. The display was eventually closed down in the 1980's, and a sign was placed outside it reading,

"A lot has happened since this exhibit opened in 1974. The science of human evolution is a fast-changing field. Much of the material here is now out of date. We are developing a new exhibit based on the latest findings."

It never re-opened.

In 1999, Colin Patterson, one of the world's leading evolutionary palaeontologists, based at the British Museum of Natural History, wrote the landmark book, *"Evolution"*. In it he failed to mention a SINGLE evolutionary transitional form. When a Christian scientist, Luther D. Sunderland, wrote and asked why he had failed to mention any transitional forms, Patterson wrote back, saying,

"*I fully agree with your comments on the lack of evidence of evolutionary transitional forms. If I knew of any (either fossil or living) I would certainly have included them in my book. I'll lay it on the line – there is NOT ONE SUCH FOSSIL [emphasis mine] for which there is a watertight argument.*"[30]

This now famous quote has severely embarrassed evolutionists, and Patterson, under pressure from the atheist movement, has subsequently tried to qualify his original comment.

If evolution was true, we should expect to find MILLIONS of transitional forms all over the earth. Yet there is not one such transitional fossil! As Prof. E.H. Andrews states, *"The fossil record now constitutes a severe embarrassment to the theory of evolution."*[31]

THE PROBLEM OF IRREDUCIBLE COMPLEXITY

Cells were once thought to be simple building blocks of life, but we now understand that this is not so. Cells are incredibly complex. Even the simplest cell is full of hundreds of molecular machines, each of which is comprised of dozens of independent parts, formed by the construction of DNA and RNA chains, each of which was constructed by other molecular machines inside the cell. And all of these machines have to exist simultaneously in order for a single cell to function and remain alive. The simplest of cells is unbelievable complex! Evolutionary theory has no way of explaining how hundreds of these micro-molecular machines could spring into existence simultaneously in order to create the first living cell.

Charles Darwin once stated,

"If it could be demonstrated that any complex organ existed which could not possibly have been formed by numerous, successive slight modifications, my theory would absolutely break down."[32]

Commenting on Darwin's statement, and in the light of our recent knowledge of the irreducible complexity of cells, Dr. Michael Behe, Professor of Biochemistry at Lehigh University in Pennsylvania and a senior fellow of the Discovery Institute's Centre for Science and Culture, states,

"As the number of unexplained, irreducibly complex biological systems increases, our confidence that Darwin's 'criterion of failure' has been met skyrockets towards the maximum that science allows."[33]

If Charles Darwin was alive today, he would almost certainly concede that his theory, according to his own defined parameters, has been refuted by overwhelming scientific evidence.

THE GENETIC IMPOSSIBILITY OF MACRO-EVOLUTION

Professor Giuseppe Sermonti, a highly respected Italian biochemist, geneticist, and molecular biologist states;

"Recent discoveries in molecular biology have deeply undermined the theory of evolution. The claim of evolution – that mutations are retained and strengthened by natural selection –

is not true. What natural selection does is eliminate genetic mutations." [34]

Professor Macki Giertyche, a geneticist associated with Torun University, Poland, and a member of the Polish Academy of Dendrology, states:

"Evolution is not a science; it is a philosophy... The science of genetics shows that macro-evolution is not possible... The main argument of evolutionists is that small, positive (or beneficial) mutations occur in the reproduction cells and are retained by natural selection. These mutations are said to gradually accumulate over time until a new species is formed. Now, I am a geneticist, and I can confirm that in all the studies in all the laboratories around the world, where many generations of organisms have been observed, nowhere have positive mutations ever been observed. All mutations are either neutral or harmful - they are never an improvement. In fact, cells are programmed to protect genes from mutations, and correct the errors that occur." [35]

In November 1980, at the Natural History Museum in Chicago, a large number of the world's leading geneticists and other scientists held a seminar to consider the issue of whether the small changes in varieties, sometimes referred to as "micro-evolution", lead to the big changes necessary for Darwinian evolution ("macro-evolution"). The findings of the conference were reported in the next issue of "Science" magazine, which stated;

"The central question of the Chicago conference was whether the mechanisms underlying micro-evolution can be extrapolated to explain the supposed phenomena of macro-evolution. At the risk of doing violence to the opinions of some of the scientists at the meeting, the answer was a clear 'No'." [36]

As Dr. Ken Ham states, *"If they had known about genetics in Darwin's day, the theory of evolution would never have gotten off the ground."*[37]

MITOCHONDRIAL EVE

In 1979, Drs Alan Wilson and Rebecca Cann published the findings of their study of female mitochondrial DNA - findings which rocked the scientific world! In order to appreciate their findings, however, you firstly need to understand a little about mitochondrial DNA. Mitochondrial DNA (or mtDNA) is a small section (16,500 base pairs) of the total human DNA chain (3.2 billion base pairs) that is contained within every cell of the human body. It is passed down from **mothers** to both sons and daughters, but sons cannot pass along their mtDNA to their children. This is because mtDNA is only transmitted through the female egg. In other words, you inherited your mtDNA exclusively from your mother.

Now, back to those findings. Drs Wilson and Cann's study of female mtDNA revealed something extraordinary and unexpected; every woman in the world is descended from a single female progenitor (genetic ancestor)! Their study of the mtDNA sequence in women from all around the world revealed the astonishing fact that there was a single, original female, from which all women alive today are descended! Their initial findings were published in scientific journals in 1979 and created a furore among atheistic scientists. Two subsequent scientific papers were published by dissenting scientists, in 1981 and 1983, which cast doubt upon the original findings. Drs Wilson and Cann responded to these criticisms by undertaking further research. They subsequently published the results of a more detailed study in 1987, confirming their original findings. Wilson and Cann's discovery was finally, and reluctantly, accepted by the scientific community. The genetic evidence is now considered to be unequivocal; all women alive today are descended from a single original woman! (The same cannot be proven for men, because of the nature of mtDNA).

This stunning scientific discovery was published in "Nature" and Science" magazines in early 1987, and the original female progenitor was given the colloquial name, *"Mitochondrial Eve"*. The news quickly spread beyond the scientific world. Articles appeared in Newsweek and National Geographic magazines, the latter entitled *"Mankind Meet Your Mother"*. A Discovery Channel documentary was also produced in 2002, entitled, *"The Real Eve: Five Billion People From One Woman"*.

The Wikipedia entry on Mitochondrial Eve reads,

"Shortly after the 1987 publication, criticism of its methodology was published. Although the original publication did have analytical limitations, the findings have since proven robust. The name Mitochondrial Eve alludes to biblical Eve."

Subsequent studies have been conducted on the male Y Chromosome, which is inherited patrilineally (passed on from father to son). A similar discovery has been made regarding the existence of a single male progenitor, labelled Y-Chromosomal Adam. It is now apparent that all males who are alive today can be traced back to a single male progenitor as well! In my book, *"No More Monkey Business: Evolution in Crisis"*, I have outlined the various imaginative explanations proposed by evolutionists to account for these astonishing facts. While Mitochondrial Eve and Y-Chromosomal Adam do not unequivocally "prove" the biblical account, they are certainly consistent with it. Furthermore, the creationist explanation is a much simpler, neater explanation of the facts than the various evolutionary explanations.

At the turn of this new millenium, in response to the mounting scientific evidence contradicting the theory of evolution, many of the world's leading scientists began to call for a symposium to determine the ongoing validity of the theory. As a response, in 2002, an international organisation of scientists was formed, called CESHE (Cercle d'études Scientifique et Historique), headquartered in France. It was a voluntary organisation comprised of many highly respected scientists, whose purpose was to determine whether the theory of evolution can still be considered to be a valid scientific theory. After a period of intense scrutiny and rigorous evaluation of all the evidence, this was their conclusion:

"The theory of evolution is not supported by science. Many scientists have accepted the theory because they assume it to be an established scientific fact. Those scientists who have investigated it, however, find that evolution is a belief, not a science." [38]

In his book, *"God, Science and Evolution"*, Prof. E.H. Andrews wrote;

"Speaking as a scientist, I believe that in another 20 years the theory of evolution will have been totally discredited, purely on scientific grounds. The enormous gaps in the theory are beginning to emerge – not, of course, in the popular versions of evolution, but in the findings of scientists who are studying these matters at depth.... The popular impression is given that evolution is scientifically proven. This view is terribly biased and ignores the yawning chasms in the theory which make it unacceptable to me as a scientist." [39]

Reflection Questions

1. What new insights have you gained from this chapter? Has this chapter changed any of your views?

2. What questions or challenges has this chapter raised for you?

3. Read Genesis Chapter 1. What inconsistencies exist between this account and the theory of evolution?

4. Read Romans 5:12. According to this verse, when did death enter our world? How is this different from the theory of evolution?

5. Read Acts 17:26 and Genesis 3:20. How do these verses contradict the theory of evolution?

6. Read the genealogies in Matthew 1:1-16 and Luke 3:21-38. Both of these passages trace the ancestry of Jesus back to Adam. How is this inconsistent with the theory of evolution?

7. Do you think there is any way to reconcile the Bible and evolutionary theory?

8. Read Romans 1:18-23. What application does this passage have for a discussion of God and evolution?

THIRTEEN

FINDING GOD AT THE CROSS

For those who are earnestly searching for God, you will find Him at the cross. The presence of God may be glimpsed in many of the events of human history, but never more obviously than in the terrible events that took place on a hill called Golgotha over 2,000 years ago. The crucifixion of Jesus is the most extraordinary event in human history. It divides the history of our planet into two epochs; B.C. (Before Christ), and A.D. (Anno Domini - Latin for "in the year of our Lord"). The cross represents God's most dramatic and unequivocal intervention into human history. And it does represent true history; not mere myth or fable. In Chapter 5, I documented the independent historical corroboration of the crucifixion of Christ, including the supernatural events that accompanied it (see quotes later in this chapter as well). The cross demands our attention, for it cries out in the most dramatic fashion that God has visited our planet and interacted with us in the most profound way.

THE CROSS AND THE LOVE OF GOD

"This is love: not that we loved God, but that He loved us and sent His Son as an atoning sacrifice for our sins." (1 Jn 4:10)

"God demonstrates His own love for us in this: While we were still sinners, Christ died for us." (Romans 5:6-8)

That the Creator of the universe should take on human form and die for His creatures is truly extraordinary. It is shocking love. It is extravagant love. We may have many unanswered questions about a variety of things that we would like to ask God. We may question why He allows so much suffering in our world. We may ask why He does not intervene in certain circumstances. We may wonder how He will judge those who have not heard about Jesus. There are many things that we may be unsure of, but we can be absolutely certain of His love for us.

"For God so loved the world that He gave His only Son, that whoever believes in Him should not perish, but have eternal life." (John 3:16).

That God should choose to die in order to save His creatures, is akin to a human becoming an ant and dying for the ants in order to somehow save them. It is unfathomable! It is outrageous! One might (foolishly) question God's sanity, but, surely, no one can question the depth of His love. That God chose such a drastic course of action in order to save us, also reveals the serious nature of sin and the unavoidability of Hell.

THE CROSS AND THE UNAVOIDABILITY OF HELL

The extreme measure of the cross surely indicates that the existence of Hell is both unavoidable and necessary. If it were not, if there was some way around the need for a Hell, some possible alternate universe that could have been created where there was no necessity for a place of final punishment, then God would have created such a world and would not have deemed it necessary to die on the cross. The fact that God did not create such a world tells us either that a universe without a Hell would be meaningless (for it might necessitate the non-existence of free will and, therefore, the complete absence of true, unfettered love), or completely illogical and unjust (a place where the laws of cause and effect, action and consequence, choice and accountability do not operate). Either way, we can only discuss the universe that did come into existence, and in this universe, there remains the necessity of an ultimate means of dealing with people who refuse to cease their rebellion against their Creator. Such people do not wish to be restored to their Creator and have no desire to be part of His eternal Kingdom. At that point, Hell becomes God's only alternative, for, as we have seen in previous chapters, He is a just God who cannot allow evil to go unpunished.

Although the cross neither explains nor justifies the existence of Hell (for Hell follows invariably from several factors that have been examined in detail in previous chapters), it does, however, powerfully illustrate the unavoidability of Hell. One can only surmise that if there was any possible means of simultaneously doing away with Hell and avoiding going to the cross, God would have done so.

As distasteful as the concept of Hell is to us, the cross is the supreme indicator of how abhorrent Hell is to God. For the cross is an extreme measure; God's ultimate, desperate means of rescuing some people from judgment and eternal annihilation. In order to save a remnant of humanity from the punishment of Hell, the Creator of the universe was willing to sacrifice Himself on the cross, an inconceivably shocking act of self-sacrifice that reveals the depth of God's repugnance at the idea of any of His creatures suffering torment and final destruction in Hell.

"As surely as I live, declares the Sovereign Lord, I take no pleasure in the death of the wicked, but rather that they turn from their ways and live. Turn! Turn from your evil ways! Why will you die, people of Israel?" (Ezek 33:11)

THE CROSS AND THE PUNISHMENT OF HELL

The Bible indicates that Jesus went through Hell for us on the cross, so that we would never have to. There is a divine mystery to this, however; one that we will never fully understand. How did Christ's death provide the means of our forgiveness? What was the exact nature of the spiritual transaction that took place as Jesus died? How did His death pay for my sins, and not only mine, but the sins of all who now follow Him?

I know the Biblical answers to these questions, but I don't truly understand them, and I don't think any human being can ever truly understand them. You see, there is a difference between knowing and understanding. I know that my wife loves me, but I don't understand why! Scientists know that gravity is the attractive force between all objects of mass, and that it can be quantified as $F = Gm_1m_2/r^2$, but no one really understands it. We can measure it, but we have no significant understanding of why mass attracts mass. This is true of all the universal laws and constants within science. We know about them, and we can define and measure them, but we simply don't understand why and how they operate as they do.

The same is true with the cross of Christ. There are things we know about Christ's substitutionary death, because the Bible tells us so:

- 1 Pet 2:24 *"He Himself bore our sins in His body on the cross, so that we might die to sins and live for righteousness; by His wounds you have been healed."*
- Col 1:20 *"And through Him to reconcile to Himself all things, whether things on earth or things in Heaven, by making peace through His blood, shed on the cross."*
- 1 Pet 3:18 *"For Christ died once for sins, the righteous for the unrighteous, to bring you to God."*
- 1 John 2:2 *"He is the atoning sacrifice for our sins, and not only for ours but also for the sins of the whole world."*
- Isaiah 53:5-6 *"But He was pierced for our transgressions, He was crushed for our iniquities; the punishment that brought us peace was on Him, and by His wounds we are healed. We all, like sheep, have gone astray, each of us has turned to our*

> *own way; and the Lord has laid on Him the iniquity of us all."*

I know all of these verses very well, in fact I could recite most of them by heart, but the nature of the spiritual transaction that took place while Christ was on the cross remains a mystery. We are simply not told how a few hours of suffering equates to the forgiveness of billions of people; we aren't privy to the calculations behind that particular equation. All we know is that during the six hours from 9:00 am to 3:00 pm, as Christ hung on the cross, He paid for the sins of the world – every sin that had ever been committed and every sin that will be committed until the end of history. For six long hours Jesus endured the full fury of God's wrath, as He was punished in our place; as if He, Himself, had committed those sins. In 2 Corinthians 5:21, Paul writes, *"God made Him who had no sin to be sin for us, so that in Him we might become the righteousness of God."* As He died on the cross, Jesus became full of our sin, and was punished accordingly. In fact, so dreadful was God's punishment upon His Son, that the Gospels record a supernatural darkness coming over the whole land from 12 noon until Jesus' death at about 3:00 pm, accompanied by a massive earthquake that split rocks and opened tombs. The darkness and the earthquake are not only recorded by the Gospel writers, but are corroborated by Thallus, a 1st century Greek historian who was not a Christian, and reasserted several decades later by the second century Roman orator and historian, Africanus:

> *"On the whole world there pressed a fearful darkness, and the rocks were rent by an earthquake, and many places in Judea and other districts were thrown down. Thallus calls this dark-*

ness an eclipse of the sun in the third book of histories, without reason it seems to me."¹

Phlegon of Tralles, a second century Greek historian, also recorded the supernatural darkness, accompanied by earthquakes felt in other parts of the Empire during the reign of Tiberius (probably that of 29 AD). He wrote;

"There was the greatest eclipse of the sun and it became night in the sixth hour of the day so that stars even appeared in the heavens. There was a great earthquake in Bithynia, and many things were overturned in Nicaea." ²

Clearly, something dreadful and supernatural was occurring as Jesus was being crucified. We cannot imagine the exact nature of Christ's suffering while on the cross, but that it involved complete separation from God the Father is implied by His heart-wrenching cry, *"My God, my God, why have you forsaken me?"* (Matt 27:46). Nor do we understand the mechanism that enabled Christ to identify the exact moment when the sins of the world had been fully paid for, but that He did perceive that moment is indicated by His final words, as recorded by John, *"It is finished"* (John 19:30). His use of the Greek "τετέλεσται" (tetelestai) at this point is significant, as it was a word commonly used in the business world to mean *"paid in full"*. The punishment for our sins was paid in full. Recompense had been made. Divine punishment, in all its fury, had been carried out, and God's justice was satisfied.

Christ went through Hell for us on the cross, so that we might never have to. While we don't completely understand how this is so, we rest securely in the knowledge that it is so.

THE CROSS AS THE ULTIMATE REVELATION OF GOD'S CHARACTER

The cross speaks of God's undeniably great love. It is the ultimate defence of God's character, providing an irrefutable response to those who ignorantly accuse Him of cruelty or indifference. Jesus, in speaking of His impending sacrifice, described it as a supreme act of love; *"There is no greater love than this; that a man should lay down his life for his friends"* (John 15:13). The extraordinary nature of this love is further revealed by the fact that Christ's sacrifice was not that of a friend for a friend, but of a God for His enemies:

"You see, at just the right time, when we were still powerless, Christ died for the ungodly. ⁷ Very rarely will anyone die for a righteous person, though for a good person someone might possibly dare to die. ⁸ But God demonstrates His own love for us in this: While we were still sinners, Christ died for us... ¹⁰ For while we were God's enemies, we were reconciled to Him through the death of His Son" (Rom 5:6-10)

Does God care that people are going to Hell? Does He love us at all? These questions are answered irrefutably by the cross:

"For God so loved the world that He gave His one and only Son, that whoever believes in Him shall not perish but have eternal life." (John 3:16)

We must concede that our understanding of Hell is foggy at best. We perceive the reasons behind its necessity only dimly, unable to comprehend with our rudimentary three-dimensional brains the trans-dimensional, metaphysical realm and the infinite wisdom of a transcendent God. The nature of Hell, and its necessity, will remain unclear to us as long as we draw breath in this fallen world. But an important principle of Biblical interpretation is to always interpret the unclear through the lens of the clear. And the cross of Jesus is abundantly clear. While the issue of Hell may continue to generate questions for some people regarding the goodness of God, these questions are irrefutably answered by the unequivocal demonstration of God's love in the sacrifice of His Son on the cross for our forgiveness. The cross gives us unshakeable confidence in the goodness and love of God; confidence that allows us to face those questions that remain unanswered with faith and trust in the God who has already proved His character to us.

THE CROSS AS THE ULTIMATE INDICTMENT

I cannot finish this chapter without a final plea to the seeker who has not yet begun a relationship with God. The God who created you has sacrificed Himself on the cross to redeem you; to forgive your sins and win back your love and allegiance. The cross demands a response from each of us. We cannot remain neutral; either we fall on our knees before the Saviour, repenting of our sins and pledging to follow Him, or we turn our backs on Him and continue to live our self-determined lives. The Bible's most well-known passage outlines these two clear choices and their eternal consequences:

"For God so loved the world that He gave His one and only

Son, that whoever believes in Him shall not perish but have eternal life. For God did not send His Son into the world to condemn the world, but to save the world through Him. Whoever believes in Him is not condemned, but <u>whoever does not believe stands condemned already</u> because they have not believed in the name of God's one and only Son. This is the verdict: Light has come into the world, but people loved darkness instead of light because their deeds were evil." (John 3:16-19)

On the Day of God's Judgment, those who have not responded to Jesus with faith and repentance, who have treated Him either with disdain or indifference, will face the fury of God's wrath. God will effectively say to them, *"What are you doing here unforgiven? Why did you not respond to my offer of forgiveness? Why did you turn your back on my Son? I have done everything I could for you! I revealed myself to you in the beauty of creation. I whispered to you in the quite of your conscience. And I died for you on the cross of Calvary!"* On the Day of Judgment, the cross of Jesus will become the ultimate indictment for those who have not heeded its message, for what more could God have possibly done?

Jesus reveals the stark contrast in what will be said to the saved and the unsaved on the Day of Judgment. To those who have responded in faith and repentance, He will say, *"Come, you who are blessed by my Father; take your inheritance, the kingdom prepared for you since the creation of the world."* (Matt 25:34). To those who continue to treat Him with disdain or indifference, He will say, *"Depart from me, you evil-doers, for I never knew you!"* (Matt 7:23).

A PRAYER OF REPENTANCE AND FAITH

It may be that in the course of reading this book you have come to believe in the truth of the Christian message, and you sense God's Spirit calling you to turn back to your Creator in faith and repentance. If that is the case, I urge you to do that right now. I invite you to pray the following prayer:

"Dear God, I confess that I am a sinner who has rebelled against You in thought, word and deed, sometimes consciously, sometimes unthinkingly. I acknowledge that I have lived my life without any meaningful reference to You, my Creator. Please forgive me. I acknowledge that You are the God of the universe and my rightful King, and I submit my life to Your Sovereign rule now. Lord Jesus, I believe You are the Son of God. I believe You died on the cross to forgive my sins and rose from the dead to be declared Lord of all. I trust You now as my Saviour and I submit to You as my Lord. I open my heart to You and ask that You will come into my life, fill me with Your presence, and strengthen me to follow You all the days of my life. Amen."

If you did sincerely pray this prayer, then I urge you make contact with a church in your area so that you can receive help and encouragement as you continue your Christian walk. You will also find on my website, SmartFaith.net, many helpful articles and resources to assist you as you continue your journey of faith.

To those who have not yet reached the point where they are ready to turn to Christ in faith and repentance, I urge you to not give up your search for the truth. Keep asking questions. Keep reading. Talk to Christians about their faith. But most importantly, do not pursue knowledge about God as some kind of intellectual quest, or in order to satisfy your curiosity; you must seek God with all your heart, for only then will you truly find Him.

"You will seek me and find me, when you seek me with all your heart. I will be found by you, declares the Lord." (Jeremiah 29:13-14)

Reflection Questions

1. What new insights have you gained from this chapter? Has this chapter changed any of your views?

2. What questions or challenges has this chapter raised for you?

3. Read Ezekiel 33:11. What does this reveal about God?

4. Read Isaiah 53:5-6 and 2 Corinthians 5:21. What do these verses reveal about the atoning death of Christ. In what sense is the atonement still a mystery to us?

5. Read Romans 5:6-10. What over-riding character of God do these verses reveal? Is there anything surprising about this?

6. Read John 3:16-19. According to this passage, why will the unsaved be condemned, and are, in fact, already condemned? What does it mean that people "love darkness instead of light"?

7. As a group, spend some time praying for friends and family who do not know the Lord, asking God to open their hearts to Him.

ALSO BY KEVIN SIMINGTON

Making Sense of the Bible

No More Monkey Business

Welcome To The Universe

ABOUT THE AUTHOR

Kevin Simington is a highly acclaimed writer whose fiction and non-fiction books have been lauded for their intelligence, wit and captivating writing style. He is a sought after keynote speaker who regularly speaks at conferences in the areas of philosophy, science and apologetics. He also writes for several magazines.

Kevin lives on the Central Coast of New South Wales, Australia, and has a wide range of interests. These include squash (he's pretty good), running (he's very fit), golf (he's very bad), surfing (he thinks he's pretty good, so let's not spoil his fantasy), bike riding, tennis and music (he plays guitar in a covers rock band). He lives on a small farm (55 acres) with his wife and his daughter and her family. Together they have 1 cat, 3 dogs, 6 sheep, 10 pigs, 12 ducks, 100 cattle, 1,800 chickens and 1 horse. Kevin's main contribution to farm work is patting the horse and the dogs.

As well as his non-fiction works, he has also written a science fiction series, the StarPath Series, the first book being, "The Stars That Beckon".

CONNECT

Visit Kevin Simington's website:
SmartFaith.net

SmartFaith.net contains a large repository of helpful resources in the areas of apologetics, theology and philosophy.

Facebook: https://www.facebook.com/kevin.simington.71

NOTES

1. Seeking Answers

1. Paul Davies, "Are We Alone", Penguin Books, 1995, pp. 149, 151-156
2. IBID

2. Evidence For Belief

1. William Lane Craig, https://www.reasonablefaith.org/question-answer/P10/is-unbelief-culpable
2. Discovery Channel Canada and National Geographic, "Falling From The Sky", 2007
3. IBID
4. http://www.jdmoyer.com/2011/07/25/why-as-an-atheist-i-pray/
5. https://www.christian-faith.com/words-of-dying-atheists-and-skeptics/
6. IBID
7. IBID
8. IBID
9. Sam Harris, "Letter To A Christian Nation", Bantam Press, p. XIV
10. Bertrand Russell, 1948 BBC radio debate, "The Existence of God", with Fr. Frederick C. Copleston
11. https://www.physicsoftheuniverse.com/scientists_friedmann.html
12. https://starchild.gsfc.nasa.gov/docs/StarChild/questions/redshift.html
13. https://www.space.com/25945-cosmic-microwave-background-discovery-50th-anniversary.html
14. http://www.picassodreams.com/picasso_dreams/2016/05/the-top-30-problems-with-the-big-bang.html
15. Stephen Hawking, Lecture: "The Beginning of Time", http://www.hawking.org.uk/the-beginning-of-time.html
16. Robert Jastrow, "A Scientist Caught Between Two Faiths," Christianity Today, August 6, 1982.
17. Robin Collins, "A Scientific Argument for the Existence of God: The Fine-Tuning Design Argument." in Michael J. Murray, editor, Reason for the Hope Within (Grand Rapids, Mich.: Eerdmans, 1999), p.48.

18. Dr. Paul Davies, "Answering Richard Dawkins", https://godandsoul.wordpress.com/tag/paul-davies/
19. http://www.growingupotaku.com/2012/12/universal-constant-proven-to-be.html
20. Fred Hoyle, "The Universe: Past and Present Reflections", Annual Reviews of Astonomy and Astrophysics, 1982, p.16.
21. Charles Darwin, "The Autobiography of Charles Darwin", Norton, 1958, pp.92-93
22. Richard Dawkins, "The Blind Watchmaker", Norton & Co, 1986, p.133
23. Fyodor Dostoevsky, "The Brothers Karamazov" (1880), Part 4, Book 11, Chapter 4
24. Jeremy Rifkin, "Algeny", Viking Press, New York, 1983, p.244
25. Michael Ruse, *Darwinism Defended*, London: Addison-Wesley, 1982, p. 275

3. The God Who Hides

1. Quoted in https://thei535project.wordpress.com/2015/04/23/not-enough-evidence-god-not-enough-evidence/
2. Carl Sagan, "Contact", quoted in https://probe.org/why-isnt-the-evidence-clearer/
3. Bruce Russell, Review of "The Elusive God; Reviewing Religious Epistemology", by Paul K. Moser, Cambridge Press, 2008
4. Hugh Ross, "Beyond The Cosmos", Reasons To Believe, 2010
5. Neil Carter, quoted inpatheos.com/blogs/godlessindixie/2014
6. https://www.youtube.com/watch?v=u9CC7qNZkOE
7. Flavius Josephus, The Antiquities of The Jews, 18.3.3 §63
8. Josh McDowell, "Evidence That Demands A Verdict", Thomas Nelson Inc, 1979
9. Frank Morrison, "Who Moved The Stone", Zondervan Press. 1930 (latest edition 2002)
10. Lee Strobel, "The Case For Christ", Zondervan Press, 1998

4. The God Who Wants To Be Found

1. https://billygraham.org/story/the-tree-stump-prayer-where-billy-graham-overcame-doubt/

5. The Historicity Of Jesus And The Bible

1. Neil Carter, quoted in patheos.com/blogs/godlessindixie/2014
2. Dr. Bart Ehrman in an interview on "Infidel Radio", https://www.youtube.com/watch?v=u9CC7qNZkOE
3. "Myth Growth Rates and The Gospels", http://www.bibleinterp.com/articles/2013/kom378030.shtml
4. Cornelius Tacitus, "Annals" (written ca. AD 116), book 15, chapter 44
5. Suetonius, "Lives of the Twelve Caesars", 121 AD
6. Africanus, quoting Thallus (96 AD), https://en.wikipedia.org/wiki/Thallus_(historian)
7. Tertullian, "Apologeticus", (197 AD), quoted in https://en.wikipedia.org/wiki/Crucifixion_darkness
8. Plegon of Tralles, quoted by Origen of Alexandria (182-254 AD), in Against Celsus (Book II, Chap. XIV),
9. IBID
10. BT, Sanhedrin 43a, quoted in https://en.wikipedia.org/wiki/Yeshu#Yeshu_the_sorcerer
11. IBID
12. Flavius Josephus, "Antiquities of The Jews", 18.3.3 §63
13. "The Testimonium Flavianum", http://www.josephus.org/testimonium.htm
14. William Ramsay, "The Bearing of Recent Discovery on the Trustworthiness of the New Testament" (1915)
15. William Ramsay, St Paul the Traveller and the Roman Citizen, 1895. Ramsay published a total of 18 further books and dozens of academic articles defending the historicity of the New Testament documents.
16. Listed in https://en.wikipedia.org/wiki/William_Mitchell_Ramsay
17. Josh McDowell, "Evidence That Demands a Verdict", Thomas Nelson; Rev. ed. 1992
18. C. S. Lewis, "Surprised By Joy", Ch. 14, p. 266
19. https://www.josh.org/faithful-transmit-old-testament/
20. http://www.khouse.org/articles/2011/960/

6. The Problem Of Suffering

1. John Stott, "The Cross of Christ", IVP, 2006, p.303
2. Epicurius, 341-270 BC
3. David Hume, "Dialogues Concerning Natural Religion", Bobbs-Merrill, Indianapolis, 1980, p.198

4. C.S. Lewis, "The Problem Of Pain", Clays Ltd, St. Ives, 1940, p.18
5. IBID, p. 25
6. A.W. Tozer, The Alliance Tozer Devotional, 27 February, 2018, cmalliance.org/devotions/tozer?id=1100
7. C.S. Lewis, op. cit. p.28
8. C. S. Lewis, "The Problem of Pain", 1940; reprinted Harper, San Francisco, 2001, p.91
9. https://en.wikipedia.org/wiki/Chaos_theory
10. William Lane Craig, "Hard Questions, Real Answers", Crossway Books, 2003, p.93
11. *David Bentley Hart, "Tsunami and Theodicy", First Things, March 2005, p.151.*
12. *David Bentley Hart, "Tsunami and Theodicy", First Things, March 2005, p. 82*
13. David Bentley Hart, "Tsunami and Theodicy", First Things, March 2005, p.74
14. John Stott, op cit, pp.335-336

7. The Problem Of Hell

1. Lee Strobel, "The Case for Christ", Zondervan Press, 2000, p.455
2. Leon Morris, "The Apostolic Preaching of the Cross", Grand Rapids, Eerdmans, 1955, pp. 162, 163
3. Dr James Boice, "The Angry God – A Biblical Exposition of Romans 1:18", monergism.com/"-angry-god"
4. J.I Packer, "Knowing God", Downers Grove, ILL.: IVP, 1973, pp.134-35;
5. A.W. Pink, "The Attributes of God", Grand Rapids: Baker, 1975, p. 82
6. A.W. Tozer, "The Alliance Tozer Devotional", 27 February, 2018, cmalliance.org/devotions/tozer?id=1100
7. A.W. Tozer, op. cit.
8. John MacArthur, "James: Guidelines For A Happy Christian Life", Nelson Books, 2007, p.30
9. John Murray, "The Epistle To The Romans", Eerdmans, 1997, p.35.

8. Eternal Torment Or Total Destruction?

1. Lee Strobel, "The Case For Christ", Zondervan Press, 2000, p.455
2. C. S. Lewis, "The Problem of Pain", London: Geoffrey Bles, 1940, p. 118
3. Samuele Bacchiocchi, "Immortality or Resurrection? A Biblical Study on

Human Nature and Destiny", Biblical Perspectives, Berrien Springs, MI 1997, p.193
4. http://lexiconcordance.com/hebrew/8045.html
5. IBID
6. J. Stott and D. Edwards, "Essentials: A Liberal-Evangelical Dialogue", London, Hodder & Stoughton, 1988, p. 316
7. Forward by F.F. Bruce, "The Fire That Consumes", Edward Fudge, Cascade Books, 2011
8. This is explained in detail at http://www.rethinkinghell.com/explore/
9. For further reading on the topic of annihilationism: www.rethinkinghell.com, www.jewishnotgreek.com

9. Set Up To Fail?

1. Matt Perman, "What Is The Difference Between Original Sin and Imputed Sin?", https://www.desiringgod.org/articles/what-is-the-difference-between-original-sin-and-imputed-sin
2. For example, "lexicographical enquiry comes to the conclusion that the meaning of the phrase may vary a good deal." Andre-Marie Dubarle, "The Biblical Doctrine of Original Sin", Herder and Herder, 1965, p.149

10. Love Me, Or Else!

1. http://www.growingupotaku.com/2012/12/universal-constant-proven-to-be.html
2. John Piper, "Desiring God", Multnomah Books, 2011, p.44
3. Jonathon Edwards, "The Works of Jonathon Edwards" Volume 1
4. John Piper, "Why Did God Create The World?", https://www.desiringgod.org/messages/why-did-god-create-the-world
5. C.S. Lewis, "Reflections On The Psalms", Geoffrey Bles Ltd, 1958, p.147

11. Christians Behaving Badly

1. Michael Coulter, "Sunday Age", Editorial, 12/5/2012
2. https://www.firstthings.com/blogs/firstthoughts/2010/03/the-truth-about-the-crusades
3. IBID
4. Dr. Edward Peters, Professor, University of Pennsylvania, "Inquisition", Berkeley, University of California Press, 1989

5. Prof. Henry Kamen, University of Wisconsin, "The Spanish Inquisition: A Historical Revision", New Haven: Yale University Press, 4th revised edition, 2014.
6. Prof. Henry Kamen, op.cit., p.60
7. Dr. Edward Peters, op.cit., p.87
8. https://en.wikipedia.org/wiki/List_of_sexually_active_popes
9. "The History of The Reformation", www.historyworld.net/wrldhis/PlainTextHistories.asp?ParagraphID=hnj
10. www.bbc.com.uk/history/troubles
11. Michael Coulter, "Sunday Age", Editorial, 12/5/2012
12. https://en.wikipedia.org/wiki/Capital_punishment_by_country
13. Andrew Shead, article, "Holy War: Islamic State & Israel in the Old Testament", https://www-archive.biblesociety.org.au/news/holy-war-islamic-state-israel-old-testament
14. cited in "Archaeology and The History Of Israel", 1968, and also "Is God A Moral Monster?" by Paul Copan

12. God And Evolution

1. "The Pew Forum", conducted 2007, released 2008.
2. Free Press, 2006.
3. *http://www.hawking.org.uk/the-origin-of-the-universe.html*
4. *http://www.hawking.org.uk/the-origin-of-the-universe.html*
5. *https://en.wikipedia.org/wiki/Robert_Jastrow*
6. "James Clerk Maxwell; Perspectives on His Life and Work", Oxford University Press, 2014, p.274
7. Dr Hugh Ross, "The Creator and The Cosmos", Navpress, 2001, pp.108-112
8. IBID
9. For details see: "*The NCSE, Judge Jones, and Bluffs About the Origin of New Functional Genetic Information,*" "*Do Car Engines Run on Lugnuts? A Response to Ken Miller & Judge Jones's Straw Tests of Irreducible Complexity for the Bacterial Flagellum,*" "*Opening Darwin's Black Box,*" or "*Can Random Mutations Create New Complex Features? A Response to TalkOrigins*");
10. For details, see "*Punctuated Equilibrium and Patterns from the Fossil Record*" or "*Intelligent Design Has Scientific Merit in Palaeontology*"
11. For details, see: "*A Primer on the Tree of Life*"
12. For details, see "*Convergent Genetic Evolution: 'Surprising' Under Unguided Evolution, Expected Under Intelligent Design*" and "*Dolphins and Porpoises and...Bats? Oh My! Evolution's Convergence Problem*"

13. For details, see *"The Origin of Life Remains a Mystery"* or *"Problems with the Natural Chemical 'Origin of Life'"*
14. For details, see: *"Evolving views of embryology,"* *"A Reply to Carl Zimmer on Embryology and Developmental Biology,"* *"Current Textbooks Misuse Embryology to Argue for Evolution"*
15. For details, see *"Sea Monkey Hypotheses Refute the NCSE's Biogeography Objections to Explore Evolution"* or *"Sea Monkeys Are the Tip of the Iceberg: More Biogeographical Conundrums for Neo-Darwinism"*
16. For details, see: *"Intelligent Design and the Death of the 'Junk-DNA' Neo-Darwinian Paradigm,"* *"The Latest Proof of Evolution: The Appendix Has No Important Function,"* or *"Does Darrel Falk's Junk DNA Argument for Common Descent Commit 'One of the Biggest Mistakes in the History of Molecular Biology'?*
17. John F. Ashton, "Evolution Impossible", Masterbooks, 2012
18. John Ashton, "In Six Days", Master Books, 2001
19. Robin Collins, "A Scientific Argument for the Existence of God: The Fine-Tuning Design Argument." in Michael J. Murray, editor, Reason for the Hope Within (Grand Rapids, Mich.: Eerdmans, 1999), p.48.
20. Dr. Paul Davies, "Answering Richard Dawkins", https://godandsoul.wordpress.com/tag/paul-davies/
21. Fred Hoyle, "The Universe: Past and Present Reflections", Annual Reviews of Astronomy and Astrophysics, 1982, p.16.
22. Roberto Fondi, "After Darwin; Evolutionary Criticism", 1980, p. 127
23. Stanley A. Rice, "Encyclopedia of Evolution", 2007, p.400
24. http://www.ucmp.berkeley.edu/diapsids/birds/archaeopteryx.html
25. *"Myths & Miracles"* by David C. C. Watson. Distributed by *Creation Science Foundation*
26. IBID.
27. IBID
28. IBID
29. https://australianmuseum.net.au/ardipithecus-ramidus
30. Luther Sunderland, "Darwin's Enigma", Master Books, 1998, pp.101-102
31. Quoted in "Evolution; The Lie", Ken Ham, Creation Science Foundation,
32. Charles Darwin, "The Origin of The Species", 1st edition, p.189
33. Michael Behe, "Darwin's Black Box; The Biochemical Challenge To Evolution", 1996, p.39
34. Giuseppe Sermonti, "After Darwin", 1980, p. 87
35. In the video, "Evolution; Fact or Belief?", distributed by Creation Science Foundation
36. Roger Lewin, "Science" Journal, Vol. 210(4472), 1980, pp.883-887
37. Ken Ham, "The Evolution Tapes", 1986
38. cercle d'études scientifique et historique, https://ceshe.fr/revue-sf-1.

html#p=3, also quoted in "Evolution; Fact or Belief?", Creation Science Foundation.
39. E.H. Andrews, "God, Science and Evolution". Creation Life Publishing, 1981, p.90

13. Finding God At The Cross

1. Africanus, quoting Thallus, https://en.wikipedia.org/wiki/Thallus_(historian)
2. Plegon of Tralles, quoted by Origen of Alexandria (182-254 AD), in Against Celsus (Book II, Chap. XIV),

www.ingramcontent.com/pod-product-compliance
Lightning Source LLC
Chambersburg PA
CBHW071902290426
44110CB00013B/1243